INSIGHT COMPACT GUIDE

FLORENCE

CW01651813

Compact Guide: Florence is the ultimate quick-reference guide to this fascinating destination. It tells you all you will need to know about Florence's magnificent attractions, from the Uffizi Gallery to the Ponte Vecchio, from Michelangelo's David to Brunelleschi's Duomo.

This is one of 130 Compact Guides, combining the interests and enthusiasms of two of the world's best-known information providers: Insight Guides, whose innovative titles have set the standard for visual travel guides since 1970, and Discovery Channel, the world's premier source of nonfiction television programming.

Discovery CHANNEL

APA PUBLICATIONS
Part of the Langenscheidt Publishing Group

Insight Compact Guide: Florence

Written by: Wolfgang Thoma
English version by: David Ingram
Updated by: Nicky Swallow
Edited by: Jeffery Pike
Photography by: Jerry Dennis
Additional photography by: Frances Gransden
Cover picture by: Tony Stone
Design: Graham Mitchener and Maria Lord
Picture Editor: Hilary Genin
Cartographic Editor: Maria Donnelly
Maps: Dave Priestley
Design concept: Carlotta Junger

Editorial Director: Brian Bell
Managing Editor: Tony Halliday

CONTACTING THE EDITORS: As every effort is made to provide accurate information in this publication, we would appreciate it if readers would call our attention to any errors and omissions by contacting:
Apa Publications, PO Box 7910, London SE1 1WE, England.
Fax: (44 20) 7403 0290
e-mail: insight@apaguide.demon.co.uk

Information has been obtained from sources believed to be reliable, but its accuracy and completeness, and the opinions based thereon, are not guaranteed.

First Edition 1995. Second Edition 2002
Printed in Singapore by Insight Print Services (Pte) Ltd
Original edition © Polyglott-Verlag Dr Bolte KG, Munich

Distributed in the UK & Ireland by:
GeoCenter International Ltd
The Viables Centre, Harrow Way, Basingstoke,
Hampshire RG22 4BJ
Tel: (44 1256) 817 987, Fax: (44 1256) 817 988

Distributed in the United States by:
Langenscheidt Publishers, Inc.
46–35 54th Road, Maspeth, NY 11378
Tel: (1 718) 784 0055, Fax: (1 718) 784 0640

Worldwide distribution enquiries:
APA Publications GmbH & Co. Verlag KG (Singapore Branch)
38 Joo Koon Road, Singapore 628990
Tel: (65) 865 1600, Fax: (65) 861 6438

www.insightguides.com

FLORENCE

Introduction

Places

Culture

Travel Tips

△ **Foundling Hospital (p85)** Arguably the first Renaissance building, with a fascinating social history.

▽ **Brancacci Chapel (p58)** Masolino's and Masaccio's great decorative masterpiece.

△ **Ponte Vecchio (p55)** Historical focal point of the commercial city, the Ponte Vecchio is world-famous for its rows of shops.

◁ **Duomo (p22)** Brunelleschi's magnificent dome dominates the city skyline, and the cathedral's beautiful interior is equally breathtaking.

◁ **Baptistry (p18)** This is one of Florence's most significant buildings. Its three sets of gilded bronze doors are perhaps its most striking feature.

▷ **Accademia (p78)** This gallery houses many important works, especially sculpture by Michelangelo, as well as a fine collection of musical instruments.

◁ **Uffizi (p39)**
A truly great collection of European painting, the colonnaded Uffizi houses many treasures including Michelangelo's *Holy Family*, Botticelli's *Primavera* and the 4th-century *Medici Venus*.

△ **Santa Croce (p90)**
Full of splendid works of art, this church is one of the highlights of any trip to Florence. Its glorious facade and beautiful cloister make this a very special building.

△ **Boboli Gardens (p65)**
Among the finest public gardens in Italy, the Boboli are dotted with statuary and delightful fountains.

▷ **Santa Maria Novella (p72)** This is the most important Gothic church in Tuscany. It was here that Masaccio introduced perspective into painting.

Cradle of the Renaissance

During the hot summer months, it is a struggle to walk from the Duomo to Piazza della Signoria. A mauve heat haze hangs in the air and damp crowds sway blindly past the golden buildings.

In the sacred tourist triangle of Italian cities, Florence beats Venice and Rome in popularity: more than 8 million people visit the city every year. Every second person appears to be a tourist searching for one of the city's four nude Davids. (Michelangelo's sculpture is in the Accademia but copies stand outside the Palazzo Vecchio and on Piazzale Michelangelo; Donatello's more subdued David is in the Bargello.)

Florence is arguably the most beautiful city in Italy, and certainly the most harmonious. The city was largely rebuilt during the Renaissance and maintains its elegantly rational urban design. In its heyday, in the 14th and 15th centuries, Florence was considered the most innovative artistic centre in Europe. Today, the Uffizi would be the world's greatest gallery of Renaissance art – if the city of Florence itself did not lay claim to that accolade.

Capital city
Tuscany is one of Italy's 20 administrative regions. It, in turn, is divided into 10 provinces: Florence, Pistoia, Prato, Lucca, Massa-Carrara, Pisa, Livorno, Grosseto, Siena and Arezzo. Florence is the capital of both the province and the region of Tuscany.

Opposite: rooftops viewed from the Duomo
Below: Michelangelo's David

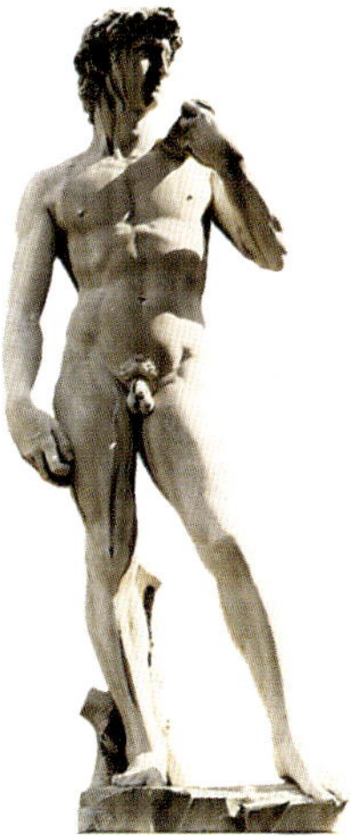

The City on the Arno

Mention Tuscany and the image that springs to mind is one of gently rolling hills covered in vineyards, olive groves and poppy fields, dotted with historic hilltop villages. But the Tuscan landscape has its wilder side. The north of the region is characterised by rugged mountains, encompassing the marble quarries of the Apuan Alps, the valleys of the Garfagnana and the ski resorts of the Apennines. To the south are the flat alluvial plains of Grosseto, as well as metal mines and power stations.

Florence (Firenze) lies at the foot of the Apennines, cut through the middle by the Arno, the principal river of the region. The city has a population of around 450,000 – though this number increases dramatically

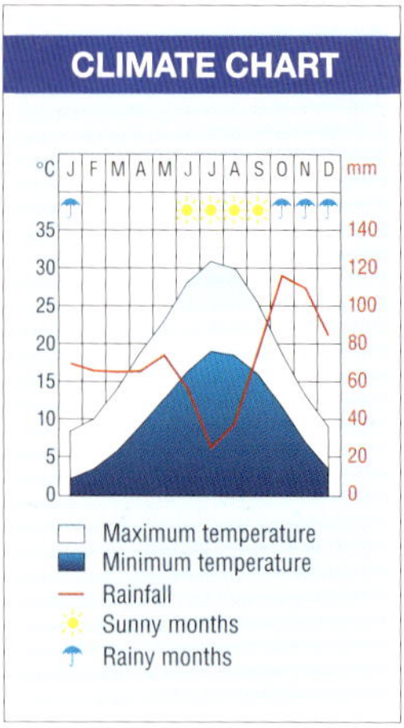

Ponte Vecchio

during the tourist season. Florence lies about 80 km (50 miles) from the sea and 50m (164ft) above sea-level. The city has the valley basin and protective chain of hills to thank for its mild climate.

Climate and When to Go

Only in July and August, when the valley is stifling and the nights prone to thunderstorms, do conditions become uncomfortable. Then it is best to follow the Florentines, if only for the afternoon, in leaving the city heat and humidity for Fiesole or any spot in the cool encircling hills.

The city seems to get more crowded each year, the peak periods being around Easter and from June to the end of August. The only relatively tourist-free months are November–February. Winters can be cold and damp, but there are a good number of cold, crisp and sunny days, and at this time of year, without the crowds, the city can be very pleasant.

Overall, the best times to visit Florence are May, September and early October, when the temperatures are pleasantly warm, but not too hot for sightseeing.

The Birth of the City

Like Rome, Florence was founded at the narrowest point of a river. It is curious to think that it all began with an administrative decision in Rome: in 59BC, an area of land was awarded to veterans of Julius Caesar's army, who founded the city of Florentia (Florence) on the banks of the Arno, overlooked by the wealthy colony of Fiesole, a former Etruscan stronghold and a site still rich in Roman remains.

Florence survived the Roman Empire but really flourished in the Middle Ages. The city's prosperity was founded on the medieval cloth trade, with imported wool processed and exported from the city. Florentine merchants controlled the market by securing trade routes, setting fixed rates of mercantile interest and getting exemption from foreign levies.

MERCHANT FAMILIES

The pace of Florence's shift from feudalism to mercantilism outstripped most cities'. This success was the product of a clear civic identity, enterprise, an enlightened view of commerce and an intuitive grasp of banking. In 1115 Florence was granted the status of a *comune*, an independent city, governed by a council drawn from the mercantile class. The merchant families settled legal disputes and, despite sharp clashes and factionalism, the common good prevailed.

The council, which eventually sat in the Palazzo Vecchio, became known as the Signoria. Today, Piazza della Signoria is still Florence's grandest square, and the Palazzo Vecchio, the magnificent Gothic town hall, remains the hub of Florentine life, the place for state banquets, traffic debates, or simply the place for ordinary citizens to renew their residence permits. Through its wealth, architectural and artistic creations, Florence had already laid the foundation for the Renaissance by the early 1300s.

URBAN EXPANSION

By 1252 there were three new bridges over the Arno, and during the decades that followed, the buildings that dominate the cityscape today were constructed. After building the Bargello, the first

Etruscan legacy
Dotted throughout Tuscany, Etruscan villages, harbours, tombs and statuary testify to a remarkable and often overlooked civilisation, to which the vitality of 15th-century Florentine art owes a great deal. Some fine examples of Etruscan art are contained in Florence's Archaeological Museum, including the celebrated bronzes, the *Arringatore* and the *Chimera.*

Below: Piazza della Signoria
Bottom: the Bargello

seat of government and the residence of the chief of police, the city commissioned the Palazzo Vecchio, a more sumptuous town hall, and the Duomo (1296), an Italian cathedral second only to St Peter's in size and splendour.

Urban expansion went hand in hand with the city's territorial gains, as Florence became the major political power of the region. By the end of the 14th century, the cities of Pistoia, Prato, San Gimignano, Volterra and Arezzo had been brought into the Florentine orbit. The capture of Pisa in 1406 brought a coveted seaport, a gain followed by Cortona (1411) and Livorno (1421). The illustrious city state of Siena stood out against Florentine domination until 1555. Lucca was the sole Tuscan city to escape absorption by Florence.

Below: Botticelli's St Augustine, *in the church of Ognissanti*

CITY OF THE ARTS

Florence thrived on artistic patronage, from the city rulers downwards. Large-scale projects were paid for by the powerful banking and wool merchant guilds, to glorify both the city and themselves. Acting on the same principle, the ruling Medici dynasty later commissioned the greatest Renaissance artists and sculptors, from Donatello and Michelozzo to Botticelli and Michelangelo.

On a smaller scale, wealthy Florentine families took great pride in the number of richly decorated

Below: the Duomo at dusk

chapels they added to the city's churches. Clues to the source of this patronage can be found everywhere in Florence. For example, on the Doors of Paradise on the Baptistry, a sack can be seen – the symbol of mercantile wealth. Profits were made then just as they are now, the difference being that the medieval mind had a guilty conscience about money-making. Charitable religious foundations helped to assuage such doubts, however, and the regular purchase of security beyond the grave allowed the arts to flourish. Thus it was that the city of the arts was founded on the guilty conscience of the merchant class.

The competitiveness of the guilds and city factions was a spur to artistic endeavour. Also at stake was the prestige of the city. The collective urban identity, known as *campanilismo* (literally the attachment to one's own belltower), fostered a unique desire to glorify Florence, to show that it was the greatest of city states. This fervour, combined with a heady intellectual climate, the re-evaluation of classical ideas, the presence of wealthy patrons and a supremely gifted pool of artists – all these strands melded in the miracle of the Florentine Renaissance.

The Medici

The rise to power of Florence's most famous family was a quiet one: the Medici did not compete for high office, but instead increased their wealth immeasurably in their role as bankers and trustees of the Church's funds in Rome. In 1397 the family moved its headquarters from Rome to Florence.

The Medici were respected by the people and feared by Florence's other grand families, above all by the Albizi. Their policy was to pull strings quietly in the background, and it was only in 1421 that Giovanni di Bicci de' Medici assumed the highest office in the Republic. Bicci's heir, Cosimo the Elder, promoted humanism and donated money to churches and monasteries, keeping a cell for himself in San Marco. He founded the Medici dynasty that ruled Florence and Tuscany as a Grand Duchy until 1737 (without a break from 1530), and included a long line of illustrious personalities.

CITY OF SCIENCE

The Renaissance was distinguished not only by a strong interest in the arts; the natural sciences exercised an equally powerful fascination. Renaissance architects Filippo Brunelleschi and Leon Battista Alberti wrote theoretical works based on their studies of the classical world. Florence was sometimes referred to as 'Athens on the Arno'. During their long reign, the Medici dynasty maintained an interest in the natural sciences alongside their penchant for art collecting. Leonardo da Vinci was commissioned to decorate their court. In 1610, Galileo Galilei discovered the moons of Jupiter with his astronomical telescope and named them the *pianeti medici,* after his benefactors. In 1545 Cosimo I, a Medici ruler, had one of the world's first botanical gardens designed for medicinal purposes.

Lorenzo de'Medici

Below: an enduring mode of transport

Below: city streets

The Florentine Legacy

As well as the discoveries made by Renaissance artists and scientists, there were major literary milestones. The Florentines were at the forefront of literary endeavour and championed the use of the vernacular. Dante and Boccaccio wrote not in Latin but in the Florentine dialect – a dialect that became recognised as standard Italian.

In the field of politics, Machiavelli's name is as relevant as ever, with *The Prince*, his manual of statecraft, a classic of the genre. In terms of banking, Florence was a world leader and devised such procedures as double-entry book-keeping. The Medici and Bardi monopolised the money markets of the day, while the first florin, named after the city, was minted in 1252 and quickly became an international currency.

Certainly, the Florentine legacy embraces artistic innovation, a revival of humanistic values, bold new scientific thinking and vivid literature. Yet the legacy is more than the sum of its parts: at its fullest, it can only be termed 'the Florentine miracle', a unique combination of circumstances that led to a flowering of the human spirit.

Florence Today

After sleeping its way through post-Renaissance social change, Florence was discovered by enthusiastic Grand Tourists in the 18th century, and the wave of arrivals has not abated. Over-exposure to enraptured visitors has confirmed blasé Florentines in their world view, one that is essentially aloof, superior and provincial. Today's population of 450,000 is happy to profit from tourism. '*Porta aperta a chi porta*' runs the local saying: 'The door is open to those bringing gifts.'

The pull of its artistic heritage risks turning Florence into 'the city with some of the finest carparks in the world'. After years of deliberation, the council introduced in 1988 a ban on city-centre traffic – this has been a partial success, despite the presence of some private cars and the profusion of (unbanned) *motorini* (scooters).

Certain far-reaching town-planning decisions

still need to be taken, however, if Florence is not to become an open-air museum. Enough residential and commercial space must be made available to keep the city's medium-sized firms and their employees from leaving. The long-term strategy is for the historic centre to remain the cultural heart, with commercial activity moved to the northwest, towards the new city airport of Peretola, and to the satellite towns of Firenze Nova and Novoli, where many administrative offices have already relocated.

Florence never became a modern industrial powerhouse. Instead, its self-confident mercantile tradition has continued, and the city has enthusiastically embraced the service sector. Apart from the tentacles of the tourist industry, Florence hosts trade fairs and congresses, and remains a noted craft centre. The Oltrarno district, on the quieter side of the Arno, is an enticing place for pottering in search of hand-tooled marbled paper, leather goods, striking jewellery or antiques.

On the chic side of the Arno, the discreet elegance of the boutiques on Via dei Tornabuoni is a sign of the highly-developed Florentine aesthetic sense. Florentine fashion still commands attention, as the names Gucci, Pucci and Ferragamo imply. World history may be made in Rome; fashion and design centred on Milan; but Florence will forever be the capital of classic good taste.

Flood-prone river
All over the city, both on the facades of buildings and sometimes inside, are little marks on the walls which indicate the level to which the Arno rose during the great flood of 1966.

Below: couture display
Bottom: fine silk

HISTORICAL HIGHLIGHTS

59BC Foundation of the Roman colony of Florentia by army veterans.

c AD250 St Miniato is martyred during the persecution of Christians under the Emperor Decius.

284–305 Florentia is the capital of Tuscany/Umbria under Emperor Diocletian.

5th century The city is repeatedly sacked by Goths and Byzantines.

541 Florence captured by Byzantium.

570 Lombards occupy Tuscany, ruling Florence from Lucca. There follow two centuries of peace, during which the Baptistry is built.

774 Charlemagne defeats the Lombards and appoints a margrave to rule Tuscany.

854 The county of Fiesole merges with that of Florence, and the city gains land.

c1000 Margrave Ugo moves his court to Florence, which soon becomes a prosperous trading town.

11th century Most of the city's churches are rebuilt.

1115 Matilda of Canossa, the last margrave, dies; Florence becomes a self-governing commune (*comune*).

1125 Fiesole is attacked and annexed by Florence.

1172 The new city wall encloses an area three times larger than before, now including the opposite bank of the Arno.

1215 The beginning of civil strife between Guelfs (supporting thePope) and Ghibellines (supporting the Holy Roman Emperor), fuelled by class warfare and family vendettas.

1238–50 The Ghibellines attain power.

1248 New town walls erected that define the limits of Florence until 1865. It is now one of Europe's richest cities.

1252 The minting of the first florin, soon the currency of European trade.

1250–60 Regime of the *Primo Popolo*, supported by the Guelfs, and now including the merchant class.

1260–6 Ghibellines in power.

1267 onwards Guelfs in power.

1283 The *Secondo Popolo*. The nobility, excluded from high political office, splits into two factions, *neri* and *bianchi* (Black Guelfs and White Guelfs).

1284 Work begins on a third city wall with 70 towers, 8 km (5 miles) long. It is not finished until 1333.

1289 Serfdom abolished.

1293 Strife between Guelfs and Ghibellines now an outright class war. The Guelfs ban Ghibellines from public office.

1294 Work begins on the new cathedral.

1299 Work begins on Palazzo Vecchio.

1339 Edward III of England defaults on massive debts incurred fighting the 100 Years' War. The two strongest banking families, the Bardi and Peruzzi, go bankrupt: Florentine economy in crisis.

1348 The Black Death reduces the city's population from 100,000 to just 45,000.

1378 *Ciompi* uprising: the wool-carder guilds and others demand a say in politics, but hold power for only six weeks.

1400–1 Competition announced to design new doors for the Baptistry.

1434 Cosimo the Elder, from the banking family of the Medici, is recalled from exile. He founds the Medici dynasty.

1439 Cosimo the Elder has the Council of Ferrara transferred to Florence.

1469–92 Cosimo's grandson, Lorenzo the Magnificent, is a wealthy Renaissance prince. Florence flourishes both economically and culturally.

1478 The Pazzi Conspiracy: Lorenzo's brother Giuliano is murdered.

1492 Death of Lorenzo, aged 44. His son Piero takes over.

1494–8 Charles VII of France invades Italy; Piero surrenders Florence to him. Medici driven from the city by the outraged citizens. The Republic is taken over by the Dominican monk Savonarola, who is burnt at the stake in 1498.

1498–1512 Niccolò Machiavelli is head of chancery; Lorenzo's son Giovanni becomes Pope Leo X, and precipitates the collapse of the Republic.

1512–27 The Medici regain control of Florence.

1527–30 The sack of Rome by Charles V's troops, and the expulsion of the Medici. Pope Clement VII brings the Republic back to Florence briefly.

1530 Emperor Charles V captures Florence and installs Alessandro de' Medici as duke; the dynasty continues to rule the city until 1737.

1555 Cosimo de' Medici captures Siena.

1569 The title of Grand Duke is bestowed on the Medici dynasty.

1610 Galileo made court mathematician to Cosimo II. Science flourishes.

1737–1859 Tuscany is part of Austria, except during the Napoleonic Wars (1799–1815).

1848 First Italian War of Independence, with Tuscany in the vanguard.

1860 Florence and Tuscany join the new United Kingdom of Italy.

1865–71 Florence is capital of Italy.

1887–1912 Tuscany remains economically buoyant, and Florence becomes a centre for foreign poets and novelists.

1919 Mussolini founds the Fascist Party.

1940 Italy enters World War II.

1944 Retreating Germans destroy three of Florence's bridges, leaving only the Ponte Vecchio.

1946 Marshall Plan aid helps rebuild the Tuscan economy and Florence establishes itself as a centre of fashion.

1966 The River Arno floods, causing immense damage. Many works of art destroyed.

1988 Florentines vote to exclude traffic from the historic city centre.

1993 A Mafia-placed bomb kills five and severely damages the Uffizi Palace.

1998 Toto Riina and other Mafiosi are given life sentences for planting the Uffizi bomb.

1: Around the Cathedral

Map on page 19

Piazza San Giovanni – Piazza del Duomo (Cathedral Square)

At the heart of Florence, the ★★★ **Piazza San Giovanni** and the ★★★ **Piazza del Duomo** still retain all their medieval splendour. The polychromatic marble used for the Baptistry, the Campanile and the Duomo creates a harmonious ensemble that still dominates the city skyline. The cathedral facade and the Baptistry have been restored in recent years.

THE BAPTISTRY

The exact history of the ★★★ **Battistero di San Giovanni** ❶ (Baptistry of St John; open Mon–Sat noon–7pm; Sun and religious holidays 8.30am–2pm) is still uncertain. Its site on the outskirts of the Roman city, the borders of which were still valid when it was built, point to the possibility of an earlier building from Roman times – according to legend, a temple consecrated to Mars, though other sources suggest a Roman governors' palace (1st century AD). Coin finds dating from the 4th and 5th centuries suggest a former church on the site that was rebuilt around the beginning of the 11th century.

Today's Baptistry was consecrated in the year 1059, but the building was not completed until the 13th century. The graceful lantern roof dates from 1150, and the rectangular western apse was added in 1202. The attic floor is also 13th-century.

The octagonal central structure, a common design for Early Christian baptistries, was decorated in a style quite out of keeping with contemporary trends. This had its reasons: during the power struggle between the pope and the emperor, the trading city of Florence preferred to remain independent, and never adopted the 'imperial' Romanesque architectural style from the north (as seen in the city-state of Pisa). The city took its architectural cue from Antiquity instead; thus the dichromatic marble exterior of the Baptistry and its formal combination of semicircles and right-

The Romanesque

Despite all its architectural alterations, for a long time the Baptistry was considered to be a Roman structure. Dante (died 1321) believed this and so did Brunelleschi (died 1446).

Since the Renaissance had such a strong and conscious affinity with Antiquity during the 15th century, the exterior of the Baptistry is referred to as 'Florentine Romanesque'. A similar architectural style is displayed by San Miniato al Monte *(see page 96)* and the Badia Fiesolana *(see page 98)*, both of which were also built in the 11th century.

Battistero di San Giovanni

angles. The green bands of marble lend movement and perspective to the white marble-clad exterior, an effect disturbed somewhat by the horizontal stripes of the angle pilasters, added by cathedral architect Arnolfo di Cambio in 1296.

Star Attraction
• The Baptistry

BAPTISTRY DOORS

The three sets of gilded bronze doors on the Baptistry are famous. The earliest, the **South Door**, is by Andrea Pisano (1330–6); it took him just six months to create and was cast in Venice. There are 28 gilded compartments, 20 of them depicting the story of John the Baptist. The pictorial representations are completely separate from their surrounding medallions, emphasising the autonomy of the composition. The theological and cardinal virtues are represented below.

The door-frame, with its plant motifs and figures, is the work of Vittorio Ghiberti (1452–62, son of Lorenzo), and the bronze figures of the *Baptist*, the *Executioner* and *Salomé* above the portal are by Vincenzo Danti (1571).

The competition in 1401 for the remaining doors was won by Lorenzo Ghiberti. It took him until 1424 to complete the **North Door**. He made use of the same form as Pisano – 28 compartments, and the same medallions – but filled it

Below: South Door detail
Bottom: John the Baptist, the Executioner and Salomé

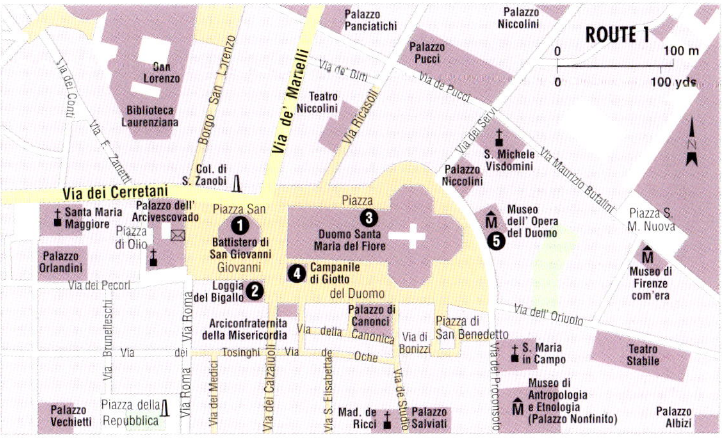

differently. Ghiberti's compositions have more freedom and movement to them, and are far more dynamic than Pisano's.

The two lower registers depict the Evangelists and Doctors of the Church. The chronological sequence of *Scenes from the life of Christ* begins on the third panel up of the left-hand door and continues towards the top, running left to right. The corners of the panels are decorated with bronze heads, one of which (fifth from the top of the left door, middle band) is a self-portrait of Ghiberti. He also did the beautiful decoration of the frame. The bronze figures above, showing *John the Baptist preaching*, *the Levite*, and *the Pharisee* are by Francesco Rustici (1506–11).

Not far from this portal a pillar erected in 1384 stands as a reminder of a legend: an elm tree is said to have blossomed on this spot on 26 January 429, while the body of St Zenobius was being carried by.

Below: East Door and detail

GATES OF PARADISE

For the **East Door** of the Baptistry, which faces the Duomo, Lorenzo Ghiberti created what Michelangelo is said to have called the ★★ **Gates of Paradise** (1425–52), a complete contrast to the South Door and his own North Door. It has 10 separate, large-format compartments, simple and

rectangular, no longer restricted to a Gothic frame, and each door is surrounded once again by continuous gilded panels. (These panels are copies; the originals are in the Museo dell'Opera del Duomo, and should be fully reassembled and displayed by 2004.) They show scenes from the Old Testament, with a sophisticated use of perspective: scenes with low relief extend far into the background, and the composition is strikingly natural. The framing contains a portrait of Ghiberti himself, looking rather mischievous [11 – *see plan*]. Above the door is the sculptural group of the *Baptism of Christ*. *John the Baptist* and *Jesus* are by Andrea Sansovino (1502), and the *Angel* was added by Vincenzo Spinazzi in 1792.

INSIDE THE BAPTISTRY

The building's interior is designed in two orders: the lower level has huge granite columns from a Roman building, with gilded Corinthian capitals, and the upper one has a gallery with divided windows above a cornice. The apse and the three portals are emphasised by double pillars and round arches extending the entire height of the walls.

The floor (12th–13th century) is decorated with mosaics showing geometrical motifs and also the 12 signs of the zodiac; the font that once stood at the centre (Dante was christened here) fell victim to the liturgical reform of the 16th century. On the right of the apse, between two columns, is the tomb of Antipope John XXIII (died 1419 in Florence) by Donatello, assisted by Michelozzo.

Donatello's famous wood sculpture of ★★ **St Mary Magdalen**, which used to stand to the left of the apse, can now be admired in the Museo dell'Opera del Duomo. The mosaics on the apse, frieze and dome were started in 1226, and the work continued until the beginning of the 14th century. Byzantine mosaicists were brought from Venice to do the work,

★

Star Attraction
- **Gates of Paradise**

Gates of Paradise
1 The Creation and Expulsion from Paradise
2 Cain and Abel
3 Noah's sacrifice and drunkenness
4 Abraham and the Angels and the Sacrifice of Isaac
5 Esau and Jacob
6 Joseph sold into Egypt and recognised by his brothers
7 Moses receiving the stone tablets
8 The Fall of Jericho
9 Saul's Battle with the Philistines; David defeats Goliath
10 Solomon and the Queen of Sheba

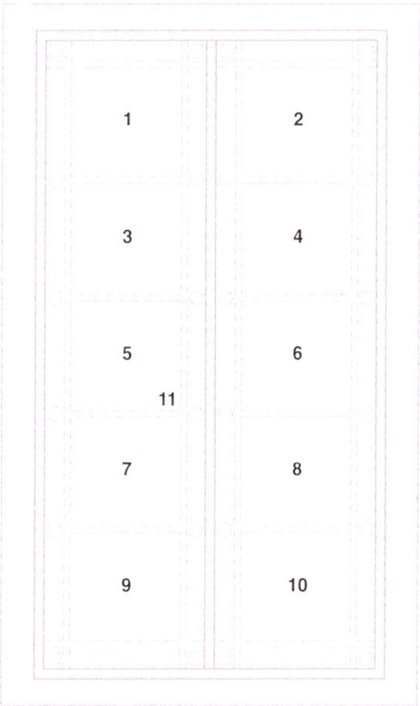

Map on page 19

Mosaic of the Last Judgement

Loggia del Bigallo

On the corner of Piazza San Giovanni and Via de' Calzaiuoli is the headquarters of a charitable institution founded in the 13th century, the **Loggia del Bigallo** ❷. The present building was constructed between 1351 and 1358, and its magnificent loggia, with its marble decor, is typical of the International Gothic style of the 14th century. Foundling children were originally left under the loggia: if they were not claimed within three days they would be sent to a foster family. The exhibits in the small museum (visits by appointment, tel: 055-2302885) include the first known pictorial representation of Florence (1345), on an icon of unknown origin, and a painted crucifix (1225–35), also by an unknown master, one of the earliest examples of panel painting in Florence.

and they passed on their skills to the local artists.

Most striking of all is the *Last Judgement*, with the huge figure of Christ, surrounded on three sides of the octagon by the medieval representation of hell. The remaining five sides of the octagon are divided into four bands, showing the story of John the Baptist, the story of Genesis (Creation and Flood), the story of Christ, and the story of Joseph. The inner band depicts the creator and the heavenly host, and vines – symbols of heavenly paradise – growing up towards the lantern above. The colour of the entire mosaic in the vault changes subtly, from the sombre tones of the Last Judgement to the bright gold of Heaven, opening up the prospect of paradise.

THE CATHEDRAL

Dominating the piazza – and the surrounding streets – is the ★★★ **Duomo Santa Maria del Fiore** ❸ (open Mon–Sat 10am–5pm; Sun and religious holidays 1.30–5pm).

After the city limits were extended in 1284, when construction work began on the third city wall, the Florentines decided that their city, which had become so powerful, needed something more representative than just the Baptistry. The new cathedral was begun after long deliberation in 1294, with the aim of outdoing such rival cities as Pisa, Siena and Orvieto – so the relevant dimensions were decided on. Master builder Arnolfo di Cambio was awarded the contract, and the foundation stone was laid on 8 September 1296.

The site was the area around the cathedral of Santa Reparata, opposite the Baptistry, which because of slow progress on the project actually remained standing until 1375. The new cathedral was renamed Santa Maria del Fiore.

CONSTRUCTION BLIPS

Construction work first came to a standstill in 1310 when Arnolfo died. It was continued only in 1334, when Giotto was hired, but he concentrated first and foremost on his campanile. Work stopped yet again after his death in 1337. Then the building work continued with a new design 20 years later, and in 1367 the final shape of the cathedral was decided. In 1378 the centre nave was given its vault, followed by the side aisles in 1380, and the choir section was completed by 1421. Filippo Brunelleschi had already won the competition for the dome in 1418, and his revolutionary construction was ready in 1436. On 25 March that year – the Florentine New Year – Pope Eugene IV consecrated the cathedral, even though the lantern was not finally completed until 1461.

The huge dimensions of the structure as a whole are most impressive. The formal language, borrowed from Antiquity, of semicircles and right-angles (of which the Baptistry is the earliest example) was retained by the Florentines right across to the apse of the Duomo, at the other end of this huge set of buildings; the breaks in style during the 15th century, though visible, have little effect on the architectural unity of the whole.

Star Attraction
- Il Duomo

THE CAMPANILE

It was on the right-hand side of the Duomo that Giotto built his ★★ **Campanile** ❹ (open daily 8.30am–7.30pm). This bell-tower was originally supposed to have been 100m (330ft) high, but Giotto's plans were altered after his death in 1337.

Below: the Duomo facade
Bottom: a side-on view, with the Campanile

Map on page 19

Below: the Campanile
Bottom: transport in the Piazza del Duomo

The only section designed by him is the lowest storey, with the portal that was added later. The ★ **bas-reliefs** (their originals are in the Museo dell'Opera del Duomo) illustrate the Creation of Man, and the Arts and Industries. They are the work of Andrea Pisano; the cycle begins on the left-hand side of the east face.

The second storey, with its rhomboid medallions, was added by Pisano after Giotto's death, and shows the Planets (Baptistry side), the Virtues (south side), the Liberal Arts (west side) and the Sacraments (north side), executed by pupils of Pisano according to his original designs. It was Pisano who added the third storey too; he designed it vertically, with embrasures in the middle. Two rows of niches run horizontally, one containing casts of statues.

Pisano died in 1348, and it was Francesco Talenti who completed the Campanile (1350–9). He added two more storeys, each with a pair of double-mullioned windows and playful Gothic ornamentation, and crowned his work with the belfry, which is as high as the two storeys beneath it, its triple-mullioned openings leading up to the cornice above.

Even though it was designed by three different architects, the Campanile is still a masterpiece of elegance: the horizontal bands at the base lend extra strength to the soaring tendency of the win-

dowed storeys – Pisano's niche storeys remain caught between the two, rather indecisively. The use of pink marble as a third colour alongside the green and white creates an impression of lightness, as does Giotto's idea of framing the tower with octagonal corner buttresses, and then lightening it further up by using large Gothic windows – despite the height of almost 85m (275ft) and the fact that the walls are over 3m (10ft) thick. The Campanile in Florence is widely considered to be the finest in all Italy.

CHANGE OF PLAN

On the recently restored southern side of the Duomo, right next to the Campanile, the change of plan in 1367 has left its traces: the outer structure of the first bay actually dates from the earliest plan by Arnolfo di Cambio.

The playful way in which it has been subdivided, with its narrow windows, small surfaces and jutting pilasters, lends it a touch of International Gothic and gives one an idea of Arnolfo's original plan for the cathedral's exterior. The change of plan in 1367, which determined four nave bays instead of three and also higher walls, disturbed the rhythmic refinement of the first version; from the second bay onwards the structuring is quite different, only allowing room for a single large window. The two different structures are unified, however, by the band of green and white marble running below the ledge. The Porta dei Canonici (Canons' Gate) **[a]** in the fourth bay *(see groundplan, page 29)* dates from before 1400, and its fine sculptured decoration was added in 1402.

CLEVER COMPONENTS

The exterior of the choir section should be seen as a cleverly structured architectural mass, from the lantern on the cupola all the way down to street-level. The enormous weight of the world-famous cupola is cleverly diffused via a series of carefully-positioned structural components: the trefoil choir with its three large apses, and

Star Attraction
- the Campanile

The Duomo's facade
For years after the cathedral was completed, no-one could make a decision on what sort of facade it should have (the Museo dell'Opera del Duomo contains models of several of the proposed versions). It was only in the 19th century that a flamboyant neo-Gothic facade by De Fabris (1871–87) was finally decided on, but this solution rather jars with the original architectural ideals involved.

Decorative detail on the Campanile

Maps on pages 19 & 29

High point
If you're thinking of climbing to the dome, it is best to do it early in the day, while you still have some stamina. There are 463 spiralling stairs to negotiate before reaching the top. But once you are there, the view of the city is fabulous.

Well worth the effort – the top of the dome

the two sacristies. The cupola has two concentric shells, the outer one being thinner than the inner one. Brunelleschi, who designed the dome, perfected the rhythm of the choir end by placing the four decorative little exedrae, with their niches and red roofs, around the octagonal drum between the three domed tribunes housing the choir chapels.

THE CUPOLA

The new plans of 1367 aimed at building a cupola that would put those of Pisa and Siena in the shade, and represent the sheer might of the city-state of Florence. The nave, the crossing and the octagonal drum were completed by 1412–3; the construction of the dome itself, however, posed several structural problems. Filippo Brunelleschi, who had won the competition for the commission in 1418, promised to construct the huge cupola – which starts 50m (160ft) above the ground – in a series of rings without the need for a wooden supporting frame.

On each of the eight sides, a master worked with a team of nine masons to construct the double-shelled dome. Brunelleschi kept an eye on the manufacture of the tiles and the composition of the mortar, organised the distribution of bread and wine for the workers, and also invented several new pieces of apparatus during construction of the dome (some of which can be seen in the Museo dell'Opera del Duomo).

TOWARDS THE BAROQUE

Under the suspicious gaze of his contemporaries, Brunelleschi's dome grew and grew. It was finally completed in 1436. Brunelleschi also designed the lantern that crowns it, but did not live to see its completion. It was only put into position in 1461. For the eight buttresses supporting the 19-m (60-ft) high temple with its eight narrow windows, Brunelleschi created decorative scrolls, which point the way towards baroque – and are also similar to the scrolls on the facade of Santa

Maria Novella (1458) by Leon Battista Alberti.

The entire structure was finally crowned in 1472 by Verrocchio's bronze ball and cross, thus finally reaching its proud height of 107m (350ft). The best view of the edifice as a whole can be obtained from just in front of the **Museo dell'Opera del Duomo** *(see page 31)*.

Star Attraction

- **Brunelleschi's cupola**

Below: the lantern casts its light into the cathedral
Bottom: detail of the dome fresco of the Last Judgement

NORTH DOOR

The stroll around the outside of the Duomo then leads to the north face, and the Porta della Mandorla **[b]** *(see ground-plan, page 29)*. It was built at the same time as the nave (1391–5), but its decorative sculpture was added in the early 15th century. The entire portal is a masterpiece of International Gothic. Several artists contributed to it: in the gable is an *Assumption of the Virgin* (1414–21) in a mandorla by Nanni di Banco, where Mary can be seen handing her girdle to Doubting Thomas. The natural gestures here already herald the Renaissance.

INTERIOR OF SANTA MARIA DEL FIORE

The three-aisled cruciform basilica is lit by high Gothic windows in the side-aisles of the second, third and fourth bays; the alteration made to the plans in 1367 did not retain the finer structuring

Maps on pages 19 & 29

Italian time
The Cathedral's astronomical clock uses the *hora italica* method of counting the hours; the last hour of the day ends at sunset or Ave Maria. This system was used in Italy until the 18th century.

Below: the astronomical clock
Bottom: Coronation *mosaic*

by Arnolfo, the first architect, and his windows in the first bay have now been filled in and can only be admired from outside. The clear formal language of the vault of the nave and the octagonal drum beneath the dome points the way towards the Renaissance, but the decorative elements are still playful Gothic – a combination characteristic of Florentine art.

Interior Details

The stained-glass windows in the nave date from when the cathedral was built and show *Scenes from the Life of the Virgin* by Donatello, Paolo Uccello, Andrea del Castagno and Lorenzo Ghiberti, who also did the three round windows. The floor (1526–1660) was based on designs by Baccio d'Agnolo and Francesco da Sangallo.

1 The most distinctive feature of the interior is the large astronomical clock beneath the mosaic portraying the *Coronation of the Virgin* (early 14th-century); the clock's face with its four heads of the prophets was painted by Paolo Uccello in 1443.

2 Tomb of Antonio d'Orso, Bishop of Florence (died 1321), a good but incomplete work by the Sienese sculptor Tino di Camaino.

3 Equestrian memorial to *condottiere* (mer-

cenary) Niccolò da Tolentino by Andrea del Castagno (1456); a variation on No 4 (below) by Paolo Uccello.

4 Equestrian memorial to *condottiere* John Hawkwood by Paolo Uccello (1436). This is a fresco giving the illusion of sculpture; newly-discovered perspective can be seen in the rendition of the plinth.

5 *Dante e suoi mondi* (Dante and His Worlds) by Domenico di Michelino (1465). Florence celebrated the 200th anniversary of the poet's birth; he can be seen holding an open copy of his *Divina Commedia*. The city panorama shows the cathedral's cupola still under construction. Dante's outstretched hand points at the three worlds of his *Commedia*: *Inferno* on the left, *Purgatorio* in the background, and above it *Paradiso*.

6 Entrance for ascent of the dome (weekdays 10am–5pm). The 463 steps here provide a good view of the inner structure of the double-shelled cupola; the inner shell is 4m (13ft) thick, the outer one only 80cm (2ft 7in). The panorama of the city from the top of the dome is most rewarding.

7 ★★ ***Pietà*** by Michelangelo (c 1550); the original is in the Museo dell'Opera del Duomo.

8 *Risurrezione* (Resurrection) by Luca della Robbia (1442–5); the portal leads to the New (or North) Sacristy. *(See Ascensione below.)*

9 High altar with bronze shrine to the city's other patron saint, St Zenobius, by Lorenzo Ghiberti, executed at the same time as the Baptistry's Doors of Paradise (1432–42).

10 *Ascensione* (Ascension) by Luca della Robbia (c 1450); the portal leads into the Old (or South) Sacristy *(See Risurrezione above.)*

11 *Angelo portacandelabro* (Angel with Candelabra) by Luca della Robbia.

Star Attraction
- Michelangelo's Pietà

A round window by Ghiberti

SANTA MARIA DEL FIORE

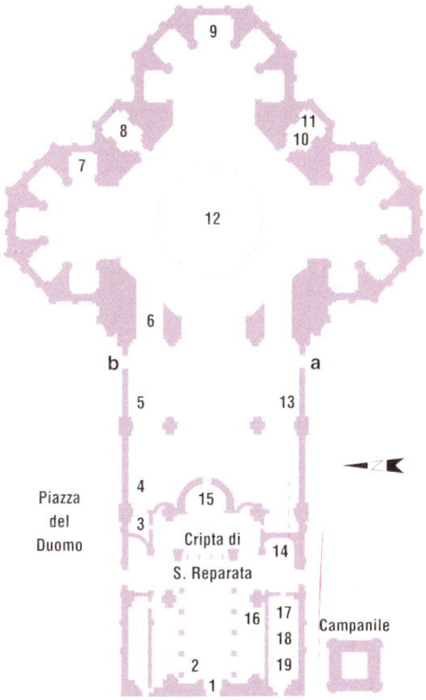

Maps on pages 19 & 29

The high altar

12 Crossing with dome. A good view here of the trefoil choir section with the three choir chapels. There is a fine view of the restored dome fresco of the *Last Judgement* by Vasari (1572–4) 50m (165ft) up, completed by Zuccari (1578–9). The three choir chapels and the drum are all octagonal, echoing the ground-plan of the Baptistry. The eight pilasters of the crossing contain statues of the Apostles by Ammannati (1565); *St James* is thought to be an early work by Jacopo Sansovino (1511–18).

13 Monument to the philosopher Marsilio Ficino by Andrea Ferrucci (1521).

14 *San Bartolomeo in trono* (St Bartholomew Enthroned) by Rossello di Jacopo Franchi (1408).

15 Excavations of the former building on the site, Santa Reparata (open Mon–Sat 10am–5pm). Santa Reparata was discovered in 1966, and in 1972 Brunelleschi's coffin was also unearthed. The ruins of this church, which was demolished in 1375, show a three-aisled basilica ground-plan with raised choir and crypt. Foundations thought to be those of a far earlier structure (4th–5th-century) were also discovered. There are several archaeological exhibits and also remains of mosaics.

16 Gothic stoup (c 1380); the original is in the Museo dell'Opera del Duomo.

17 Bust of Giotto by Benedetto da Maiano.

18 The prophet Daniel, attributed to Donatello.

19 Bust of Fillipo Brunelleschi by his pupil Andrea Cavalcanti (1447).

One Last Look

After this tour of the interior it is a good idea to take a look back inside the cathedral from the central portal: the gilt-framed panels on the first two pillars are particularly striking in the soft evening light: on the left nave pillar, *St Zenobius* by Giovanni del Biondo (1375–80) and on the right pillar *St Anthony*, prior of San Marco and Archbishop of Florence, painted by Poppi (1589).

THE CATHEDRAL MUSEUM

Since 1891, the building at No 9 Piazza del Duomo, opposite the cathedral's main apse, has housed the ★★ **Museo dell'Opera del Duomo** ❺, the Cathedral Museum (open Mon–Sat 9.30am–7.30pm; Sun 9am–1.40pm). It contains superb works of art taken from the Duomo, the Baptistry and the Campanile.

The museum reopened in early 2000 after extensive rebuilding. The layout has been improved, with access for disabled visitors. A new section has been added and some exhibits have been ordered more logically. The courtyard has been covered over by a glass roof.

Star Attraction

• Museo dell'Opera del Duomo

Historic workshop

The building that now houses the museum was built in the 15th century as the cathedral workshop, to maintain the fabric of the Duomo and commission new work, principally sculpture and furnishings to adorn the facade and interior. It was here, in the tiny courtyard, that Michelangelo carved his mighty *David.*

A TOUR OF THE MUSEUM

The museum's entrance takes you into the ticket hall and bookshop, after which the dramatic story of the cathedral facade can be followed on the ground floor. A contemporary sketch illustrates the facade by Arnolfo di Cambio, the cathedral's first architect, which was torn down in 1588. The figures planned by Arnolfo as decoration are also visible. The sculpture on display consists mostly of statues and figures created to adorn the Duomo, the Baptistry and the Campanile, from Florentine sculptors active in the 14th and 15th centuries, including Donatello and Nanni di Banco.

Below: Donatello's Cantorie
Bottom: Museum interior

Baptistry treasures The corridor from the room containing the Campanile bas-reliefs leads into a room dedicated to the Baptistry, and containing the distinctive silver altar of St John the Baptist, a fine example of the silversmith's craft which was created between 1366–1480; it originally stood in the Baptistry. The altar is Gothic, and the statuette of the Baptist in the centre niche at the front was added by Michelozzo. The reliefs showing scenes from the life of St John are almost too large for their frames. The eight scenes on the front of the altar and the two on each of its sides are the work of various artists. The *Decollazione* (Beheading of the Baptist) by Andrea del Verrocchio (1477–80) on the right-hand side is very realistically done. The striking, highly expressive wooden statue of a praying woman is the famous ★★ St Mary Magdalen, by Donatello.

Michelangelo's Pieta

Before ascending to the first floor of the museum you pass through the newly-converted courtyard where six of the original panels from the Gates of Paradise are on display, having been restored. Eventually – by 2004, if things go according to plan – the complete set and their surround will be reconstructed here.

MICHELANGELO MASTERPIECE

The half-landing on the way to the upper floor was chosen for one of the most famous pieces of sculpture in the world: Michelangelo's ★★ ***Pietà***, brought here from the cathedral in 1981. Michelangelo started the work in Rome around the year 1550 when he was roughly 75, and intended it for his own tomb, but gave it to his pupil Tiberio Calcagni as a present because the Christ figure had a broken leg. In 1722 the *Pietà* found its way into Florence Cathedral. Despite restoration, it is one of the most impressive sculpture groups in the history of art; the figure of the mourning Joseph of Arimathea (or possibly, Nicodemus) is a self-portrait.

The upper floor of the museum is dominated by the two ★★ ***Cantorie*** (choir lofts) by Donatello (1433–9) and Luca della Robbia (1432–8), which used to stand above the two sacristy doors in the Duomo. In the hall next door, the original hexagonal bas-reliefs from the lowest storey of the Campanile can be admired; the lower row is by Giotto, the upper by Andrea Pisano.

MAN AT WORK

From the room dedicated to the Baptistry a ramp leads down to the new Brunelleschi area. It contains his death mask, wooden models of his dome and lantern, various 15th-century masons' tools, a reconstruction of Brunelleschi's site when working on the Duomo and several of his architectural inventions. Also on display are the models submitted for the facade competition in the 16th century – a contest finally resolved in 1800.

2: Around the Uffizi

Piazza della Signoria – Palazzo Vecchio – Uffizi – Santi Apostoli – Santa Trinità – Palazzo Rucellai – San Gaetano – Santa Maria Maggiore – Piazza San Giovanni

From 1300 onwards, ★★★ **Piazza della Signoria** became the centre of secular power in Florence. The government building, the Palazzo della Signoria, was started here in 1299, built by the ruling Guelfs in an area formerly occupied by Ghibelline families. Ever since the Medici moved into the Palazzo Pitti in 1559, the building has been referred to as the **Palazzo Vecchio** (Old Palace). Excavations in the piazza have revealed traces of the former Ghibelline structures, as well as Roman and prehistoric remains.

The huge **Loggia dei Lanzi** forms a very distinctive part of the piazza. It was built between 1376 and 1382, designed for ceremonial and official events for the *signoria* and the townspeople. The harmonious round arches and the artistically shaped pillars they rest on represent a total rejection of the International Gothic style, a whole generation before Brunelleschi.

The medallions display the common Florentine mixture of semicircles and corners; the statues in the hall are antique and Renaissance, and the most famous ones are at the front (*Perseus* by

Star Attraction
- **Piazza della Signoria**

Below: Piazza della Signoria
Bottom: Cosimo I statue

Map on page 35

Benvenuto Cellini is left of the staircase, and Giambologna's *Rape of the Sabine Women* stands to the right).

THE SQUARE EXPANDS

Bartolomeo Ammannati's **Fountain of Neptune** (1575) and Giambologna's **equestrian statue** of Cosimo I (1594) arrived in the square long after the Loggia. It was Cosimo I who got Michelangelo to start thinking about a possible extension of the piazza. For financial reasons it retained its irregular shape, and with its exhibition of sculptures along the palazzo facade and the right-angled loggia, it resembles nothing more than a well-structured open-air museum.

The main theme here – directly derived from the fierce pride of the city-state – is 'liberty': the word *libertas* appears twice in the coat-of-arms under the projecting battlements. Donatello's *Lion* (known as the *Marzocco*), which dates from 1420 (a copy: the original is in the Bargello), can be seen holding the city's fleur-de-lys in its paw; alongside it is Donatello's group *Judith and Holofernes* (1455–60); in front of the portal, Michelangelo's *David* (1504) (a copy: the original is in the Accademia); and next to that is *Hercules and Nessos* (1533) by Bandinelli.

Cellini's Perseus
The statue of Perseus in the Loggia, newly restored and resplendent, is the original. However, the base on which it stands is a copy; the original was too badly damaged to repair.

PALAZZO VECCHIO

The ★★ **Palazzo Vecchio** ❻ (open Mon–Wed, Fri and Sat 9am–7pm, Thur and Sun 9am–2pm; June–Sept: Mon and Fri 9am–11pm) is Florence's most famous landmark, alongside the Duomo.

Cathedral architect Arnolfo di Cambio began work on this edifice in 1299, and most of it, including the 94-metre (310-ft) high tower, was completed by the year 1314. Extension work then followed at various dates up until 1592. The Italian parliament met here between 1865 and 1871 when Florence was the capital of reunified Italy; today it is the mayor's official residence, and the majestic inner rooms are used for exhibitions and concerts. The only room that provides a good idea

The Palazzo Vecchio's tower

of what most of these inner chambers must have been like originally is the *Sala d'Arme* (Weapons Hall). The entrance to this unpretentious vaulted room is on the north side of the building.

The Palazzo looks as defensive as ever, although in medieval times there was a wall the height of a man running all the way round. The distinctly Florentine divided windows only begin very high up the facade. The mighty battlemented gallery juts out, and the tower grows out of it to a height of 94m (310ft); for the bell-tower a special storey supported by four pillars was added.

Star Attraction
- **Palazzo Vecchio**

Below: column relief in the courtyard

COURTYARD AND INTERIOR

The inner courtyard *(cortile)* that one enters first was laid out by Michelozzo, who 'modernised' it between 1439 and 1454. It received its present-day decoration on the occasion of the lavish wedding of Francesco de' Medici and Joanna of Austria in 1565. Giorgio Vasari had the pillars refurbished with stucco and gold, and the ceilings painted in Pompeiian style. The walls were decorated with *vedute* of Austrian cities – much to

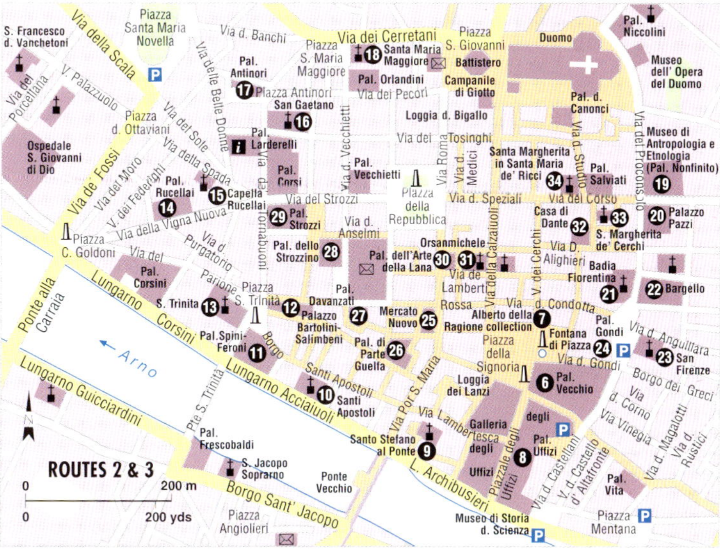

Maps on pages 35 & 37

Odd hours
You will not always be able to see all the 'public' rooms in the Palazzo Vecchio. Accessibility depends on various factors such as special exhibitions or restoration work, and sometimes rooms are used by the municipal administration.

Below and bottom: ceilings inside the palace are finished in a variety of styles

the surprise of the bride, apparently. The winged goblin holding a dolphin, on top of the fountain in the centre of the courtyard, is a copy of a work by Andrea del Verrocchio (1476).

After the Medici finally established autocratic rule in 1537, Cosimo I commissioned the art critic, painter and architect Giorgio Vasari to refurbish the palace interior.

ROOMS AND THEIR TREASURES

1 **Salone dei Cinquecento**. Modelled after the Doge's Palace in Venice, this large salon was built in 1494. Vasari transformed it in 1563–5 when the present decoration was carried out in honour of Cosimo I. It was a huge undertaking, particularly the ceiling where Vasari and his pupils glorify the Medici family and the city's history with 39 paintings in the gilt-coffered panels. The magnificent *Udienza* (audience area) [**1a**] is a raised tribuna, distinctive for its neoclassical decor, marble intarsia and statues of members of the Medici family. Among the sculptures here is Michelangelo's *Victory*.

2 **Studiolo di Francesco I**. A tiny study, with a barrel vault, decorated in the Mannerist style by the Vasari school (c 1570).

3 **Tesoretto**. A small staircase leads to the private study of Grand Duke Cosimo I.

4 **Sala dei Dugento**. The name is derived from the council of 200 persons who met here in 1441; Giuliano and Benedetto da Maiano built the hall between 1475 and 1480. The ★ **coffered ceiling** has been attributed to Michelozzo.

5 **Sala di Leone X**. The frescoes here, painted in 1560, are devoted to Pope Leo and scenes from his life. Michelangelo and Leonardo da Vinci can both be seen in the painting illustrating the *Appointment of the 21 Cardinals*. On the lower half-landing on the way up to the second floor there is a 16th-century fresco of the piazza showing the defensive wall that ran in front of the palazzo.

6 Sala degli Elementi. Vasari decorated the ceiling here with complicated allegories of the four elements: earth, air, fire and water.

7–12 The neighbouring rooms are named after the mythological themes illustrated in their paintings: the Loggiato di Saturno (Saturn) [7], Sala di Ercole (Hercules) [8], Terrazzo di Giunone (Juno) [9], containing the original of Verrocchio's winged goblin (copy on the fountain in the courtyard), Sala di Giove (Jupiter) [10] with two marvellous cabinets in pietra-dura, Sala di Cibele (Cybele) [11] with its original floor and wooden cabinets, and the Sala di Cerere (Ceres) [12].

13–18 Quartiere di Eleonora di Toledo. Vasari refashioned these apartments for the wife of Cosimo I in 1562. The Camera Verde (Green Room) [13] provides access to a tiny secret chamber in the outer wall. The Cappella [14] is adorned with frescoes by Agnolo Bronzino (1564). The following rooms were illustrated with allegories of the Female Virtues: Camera delle Sabine [15], Camera di Ester [16], formerly a dining-room, Camera di Penelope [17], a study, and Camera di Gualdrada (the Grand Duchess's bedchamber) [18].

Fresco in the chapel of Eleonora di Toledo

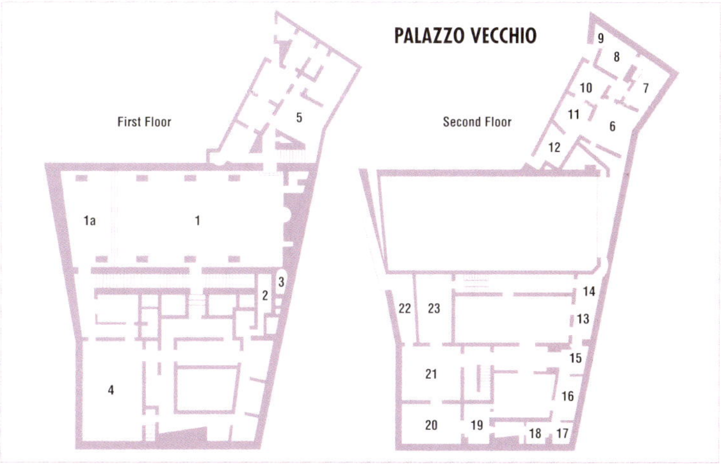

Maps on pages 35 & 37

Vasari's corridor

A passageway connecting the Palazzo Vecchio with the Uffizi Palace was built on the first floor. Then, from 1565, a corridor was constructed that led from the Uffizi across the Ponte Vecchio to the Palazzo Pitti, the home of the ruling family. This was so that the Medici could move from the Palazzo to the Pitti Palace without having to rub shoulders with the general populace. This Corridoio Vasariano (Vasari Corridor) is architecturally unique, and today contains what is probably the largest collection of self-portraits in the world. The corridor is only open during certain periods of the year according to staff availability. Call the tourist office for information.

19 **Cappella della Signoria**. The frescoes are by Ridolfo del Ghirlandaio (1514); the altarpiece is by his pupil Mariano da Pescia.

20 **Sala dell'Udienza**. The magnificent gilt ceiling and the intarsia work on the doors leading to the Sala dei Gigli, with the figures of Dante and Petrarch (c 1480), are the work of Giuliano da Maiano and his assistants. The marble portal leading to the chapel dates from the final days of the Republic (1529).

21 **Sala dei Gigli**. The golden lilies on a white background are a reminder of the Republic's futile alliance with France against the German emperor. The portal and the ceiling are by the Maiano workshop. The fresco showing St Zenobius is by Domenico Ghirlandaio (1481–5). Donatello's fine bronze statue of ★ ***Judith and Holofernes*** is also on display here.

22 **Cancelleria**. This room was used as an office by Niccolò Machiavelli; his portrait and bust are by Santo di Tito.

23 **Guardaroba**. The wooden cupboards are adorned with historic maps; the 53 panels are the work of Stefano Buonsignori (1575–84) and before him Ignazio Danti (1563–75), who also created the huge map of the world in the middle of the room.

External view of Vasari's corridor

MODERN ART

Anyone keen on contemporary Italian art should visit house No 5 on the Piazza della Signoria, which contains the **Alberto della Ragione collection ❼** (open Wed–Mon 9am–2pm). Owned by the city, this gallery contains work by Marino Marini, Giorgio Morandi, Carlo Levi, Renato Guttuso and Emilio Vedova.

★

Star Attraction
- **Uffizi Gallery**

Below: statue in the Piazzale degli Uffizi
Bottom: a view from above

UFFIZI PALACE

The Medici family ruled from the Palazzo Vecchio as absolute potentates from 1531 onwards, and when they moved into the building the municipal authorities were forced to leave. Giorgio Vasari built a new home for them: the long, U-shaped **Uffizi Palace ❽** (1560–70). He designed two storeys in Renaissance style, supported by Doric colonnades and an attic floor in between, and decorated the whole with a combination of round arches, triangles and rectangles.

The successor of Cosimo I, Grand Duke Francesco I, ordered Vasari's successor, Bernardo Buontalenti, to convert the open loggia of the administrative building into rooms for the Medici family's art collections. The loggia thus became a *galleria* enclosed in glass in 1580, and today's expression 'art gallery' is derived from it. The Medici family housed its entire art collection there, and bequeathed it to the city in 1737.

UFFIZI GALLERY

Today the Uffizi building houses the remains of the church which had to be pulled down to make way for it, San Piero Scheraggio, as well as the Gabinetto dei Disegni e delle Stampe (Prints and Drawings Collection) – one of the finest in the world. The upper floor is devoted to the ★★★ **Galleria degli Uffizi**, the most important collection of paintings in Italy, and one of the great art collections of the world (open Tues–Sun 8.15am–6.50pm).

Before your visit, take a brief stroll to get your bearings; there are fine views across the roofs

Maps on pages 35 & 41

Museum tickets

Since there's always a long queue at the Uffizi, it's a good idea to use a booking service which also schedules admission to all the other state museums in Florence (Pitti, Galleria dell'Accademia, Museo Archeologico, Bargello, etc). The service is run by Firenze Musei (tel: 055-294883) and operates weekdays 8.30am–6.30pm, Saturday 8.30am–12.30pm. Tickets can be picked up at the relevant museum, and can be paid for either in cash or by credit card at the time of booking.

Botticelli's Annunciation

of the city and of the other bank of the Arno. The corridors themselves are decorated with paintings, tapestries and antique statues.

CORRIDORS AND THEIR CONTENTS

A Corridor leading to Palazzo Vecchio.
B Administrative offices.
C Vestibule containing statues of Julius Caesar, Augustus and Hadrian.
D East Corridor. The 6th-century painted ceiling has mythological scenes, landscapes and decorative motifs. Along the walls: Flemish tapestries, and a 16th-century cycle depicting the Twelve Months of the Year.
E South Corridor. The ceiling here (17th-century grotesque) displays historical, religious and allegorical motifs. Fine antique sculpture, and a magnificent view of Florence.
F West Corridor. The 16th-century tapestries here are from Florentine workshops (Passion cycle) and also Flemish (The Story of James; various battle scenes). Antique sculptures are found along the corridor.
G Staircase leading to Corridoio Vasariano.
H Terrace, bar, WC.

TUSCAN MASTERPIECES

The collection of paintings in the Uffizi contains unique masterpieces that provide an excellent general impression of Tuscan painting, and of the way in which it freed itself from Byzantine severity and formality. This is particularly evident in the first halls, which contain works by Cimabue, Duccio, Giotto, Simone Martini, Ambrogio and Pietro Lorenzetti, Taddeo Gaddi, Bernardo Daddi, Andreo Orcagna, Gentile da Fabriano, Paolo Uccello, Fra Angelico, Domenico Veneziano, Masaccio, Piero della Francesca, Fra Filippo Lippi, Benozzo Gozzoli, Antonio and Piero Pollaiuolo – the list can only provide a hint of what should be seen here.

Rooms 10–16 contain the full magnificence of Renaissance art, with works by Sandro Botticelli (including *Primavera* and the *Birth of Venus*), Filippino Lippi, Domenico Ghirlandaio, Luca Signorelli, Lorenzo di Credi, Verrocchio, and Leonardo da Vinci; these are interspersed with works of the Flemish school by Hans Memling, Roger van der Weyden and also Hugo van der Goes, whose triptych of the *Adoration of the Shepherds*, commissioned by the Medici agent in Bruges, Portinari, had an important influence on contemporary Florentine artists.

Room 17 contains antique sculptures and also paintings by Andrea Mantegna; and Room 18 contains the famous *Medici Venus*, a 4th-century Greek statue. Central Italian painters (Room 19) and Venetian artists of the 15th and 16th centuries (Room 21) can be found on either side of the German masters Albrecht Dürer, Lukas Cranach and Hans von Kulmbach in Room 20.

German painting is again represented by Hans Holbein and Albrecht Altdorfer in Room 22, alongside works by Bellini, Carpaccio, Giorgione and Cima da Conegliano. Room 23 contains works by painters from Emilia Romagna (especially Correggio) and Lombardy as well as from Flanders.

Star Attraction
- **Uffizi Gallery**

Portrait of Eve *by Lukas Cranach*

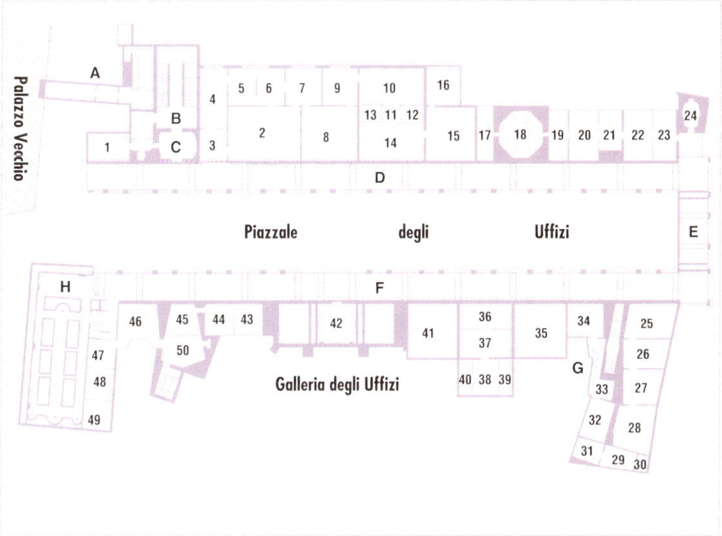

Maps on pages 35 & 41

After indulging briefly in the superb view of the other bank of the Arno from the South Corridor, Room 25 and the ones that follow it contain works by the greatest names in the history of Tuscan painting: Raphael, Andrea del Sarto, Rosso Fiorentino and Michelangelo. Room 28 has several superb works by the Venetian artist Titian, Room 29 contains paintings by Parmigiano, from Parma, and the Emilian school is represented in Rooms 30 and 31.

Room 32 has works by the Venetians Sebastiano del Piombo, Paris Bordone and Lorenzo Lotto; and Rooms 34 and 35 contain various Venetian masterpieces by Paolo Veronese and Jacopo Tintoretto. Room 41 is dedicated to the work of Flemish painter Peter Paul Rubens.

The rooms that follow, containing works by Rembrandt, Carracci and Caravaggio and also several 18th-century French and Italian paintings, are being restructured; major names here include Canaletto, Francesco Guardi, Pietro Longhi, Rosalba Carriera and Antoine Watteau.

Below: Young Girl Reading Petrarch *by Andrea del Sarto*
Bottom: Michelangelo's Study for the Battle of Cascina

MEDIEVAL FLORENCE

Via Lambertesca leads west away from the Uffizi Palace, parallel to the Arno. Even on the most crowded days at the Uffizi, this little medieval alley is usually an oasis of calm. Just before the

end of it, through an archway before the last house to the left, is **Santo Stefano al Ponte** ❾.

The medieval city, with its churches and towers, grew up along this small stretch of land between the Roman wall and the Arno, and the facade of Santo Stefano still bears traces of Florentine Romanesque *(see page 18)*, though the building as a whole was restored by Ferdinand Tacca in the 17th century. The interior (visits by appointment only, tel: 055-2710732) contains Tacca's distinctive ★ **bronze altar frontal** of the *Stoning of St Stephen*. The ★ **altar steps** (1574) at the east end, a Mannerist work by Buontalenti, are also worthy of note; the clever use of perspective here is fascinating.

Statue signposts

During the 19th century, the niches along Vasari's Uffizi Palace arcades were filled by rather unsuccessful statues representing leading national figures. You'll find the medieval alley Via Lambertesca between the sculptures of Guido of Arezzo, the inventor of the musical staff, and the goldsmith and sculptor Benvenuto Cellini.

SANTI APOSTOLI

Via Lambertesca continues into the Borgo Santi Apostoli. Medieval Florence, with its mysterious little alleyways all running off the parallel Via delle Terme, is fascinating to explore. Going back down from Via delle Terme, Via delle Bombarde leads to Piazza del Limbo (once a cemetery for unbaptised babies) in front of ★ **Santi Apostoli** ❿ (open daily 10am–noon, 4–7pm). Notice the Byzantine-style window slits above the side-aisle and the double window divided by a small pillar above the portal. An inscription on the left of the Romanesque stone facade announces that Charlemagne came here in 805, and founded the church.

The alterations the church has received since that time have been harmonious. The basilica, with its marvellous open timber roof, is divided by two sets of six Corinthian columns; the first pair were taken from the nearby Roman thermal springs, and the others are copies. The left side-aisle has a large and harmoniously structured *tabernacle* by Andrea della Robbia's workshop (15th-century). The many fine tombstones set into the floor make it clear how important this ancient basilica is to Florence; the spark that makes the cart explode in the *Scoppio del Carro* festival on Easter Sunday is carried in a procession to the Duomo from this church.

Santi Apostoli

Map on page 35

Palace of shoes

The Palazzo Spini-Feroni is one of the city's few remaining 13th-century palaces. It was once the home of the coutourier Salavatore Ferragamo, and his boutique (usually full of Japanese tourists) now occupies the ground floor. Above the shoe shop, the small but excellent **Museo Ferragamo** (open Mon, Wed and Fri by appointment only; tel: 055-3360456) is a testament to the life and work of one of modern Florence's best-known figures. Some of Ferragamo's most spectacular shoes are on display, as well as memories of his trade and travels.

ELEGANT SHOPPING

The Borgo Santi Apostoli opens up into the Piazza Santa Trinità. Here, the Roman wall coming from Via Porta Rossa makes a turn, and today's Via Tornabuoni, the most elegant street in Florence, still follows the route it took. This street looks exceptionally impressive at night, when the streetlights illuminate its facades. The piazza is dominated by the Column of Justice from the Baths of Caracalla in Rome, presented to Cosimo I by Pope Pius IV (the porphyry figure of *Justice* on the top is by Francesco Ferrucci, 1581).

THREE CONTRASTING PALAZZI

The battlemented **Palazzo Spini-Feroni** ⓫ (late 13th-century) still has the air of a medieval fortress. Ask the doorman if you can have a quick look at the grand entrance hall. Opposite, on the right-hand side of the Borgo Santi Apostoli, the **Palazzo Buondelmonti** is a perfect example of a 15th-century Florentine patrician's house, with a separate ground floor, Florentine windows with their distinctive 'eyebrows', and a loggia at the top.

On the next corner, at the junction of Via delle Terme and Via Porta Rossa, the **Palazzo Bartolini-Salimbeni** ⓬ is a clear example of the change of style that resulted from the Roman Renaissance in the 16th century: the decoration

Salvatore Ferragamo shoes

has become three-dimensional, resulting in a fascinating interplay of light and shadow across the reliefs on the facade (presently being renovated).

Below: Palazzo Bartolini-Salimbeni
Bottom: door detail at Santa Trinità

SANTA TRINITA

On the other side of the piazza is the baroque facade (by Buontalenti, 1593) of the church of ⋆**Santa Trinità** ⓭ (open Mon–Sat 8am–noon, 4–6pm, Sun 4–6pm). It is hard to believe that this church dates back to the 11th century. The three-aisled building has a transept and a raised choir; the windows are Gothic, but the side-aisles and the choir have rectangular chapels – an architectural feature typical of the mendicant orders (Santa Trinità belonged to the Vallombrosan Order). The church is noted for its interior decoration: the orders invited rich patricians to decorate the chapels and salve their consciences by serving God as well as humanity. The works of art in the 17 chapels include:

Third chapel on the right (Cappella di San Luca): altarpiece of the *Madonna Enthroned with Four Saints* by Neri di Bicci (1466).

Fourth chapel on the right (Cappella della SS Annunziata): an *Annunciation* by Lorenzo Monaco (1422).

Second chapel to the right of the main altar (Sassetti Chapel): *Adoration of the Shepherds* (1485), the alterpiece of this chapel and one of Domenico Ghirlandaio's most important works; frescoes of the *Life of St Francis* by Ghirlandaio (1483); in the lunette above the altar, *St Francis Receiving the Rule of the Order from Pope Honorius III*. Ghirlandaio chose Florence as his backdrop here: the Loggia dei Lanzi and the Palazzo Vecchio can be made out, the Uffizi did not yet exist. The bald man front-right is the merchant Sassetti, who commissioned the work, standing between his son and Medici prince Lorenzo the Magnificent. On the stairs is the poet Angelo Poliziano (Politian), the author of *Orfeo* (1475).

Sacristy (door on the left of the side exit): marble tomb of Onofrio Strozzi, by Lamberti (1421).

Second chapel to the left of the main altar (Scali

Map on page 35

Below: Palazzo Rucellai
Bottom: warning sign

Chapel): tomb of Benozzo Federighi, Bishop of Fiesole, by Luca della Robbia (1454–8).

Fifth chapel to the left (Cappella dell'Assunta): *Mary Magdalen*, a wooden statue by Desiderio da Settignano, completed by Benedetto da Maiano (late 15th-century).

Third chapel to the left (Davanzati Chapel): an *Annunciation* by Neri di Bicci (mid-15th century); the tomb of Giuliano Davanzati (1444) was adapted from a 3rd-century Palaeochristian sarcophagus (Mithras cult) with a relief of the Good Shepherd.

Crypt: the remains of the earlier Romanesque church that occupied this site.

Patrician Mansion

Via del Parione passes to the right of the church. The former monastery cloister of Santa Trinità is now a study centre for young people. Via Parioncino leads off to the right and into Via del Purgatorio, which in turn leads to the ★★ **Palazzo Rucellai** ⓮, the former home of the Rucellai family of patricians, whose name is immortalised in the facade of Santa Maria Novella.

Although the palazzo is closed to the public, its exterior is well worth closer inspection. Work began on the building in 1446, and architect Leon Battista Alberti (1404–72), with his detailed knowledge of Antiquity, lent a new dimension to Florentine secular architecture by giving it a Roman facade. The building has rusticated masonry, pilasters imitating classical orders, and graceful double windows on its upper storeys, all in perfect proportion. The transition here from medieval palace-fortress to city palazzo is complete.

Chapels and Churches

To the left of the palazzo, Via dei Palchetti and Via dei Federighi lead on to Via della Spada, and on the corner is the **Cappella Rucellai** ⓯ (Sat afternoons only), also by Alberti (completed 1467). He designed the barrel vault and added the antique decor. The former church of San Pancrazio, which adjoins the square, is now a **museum** (Mon and Wed–Sat 10am–5pm, Sun 10am–1pm, Thur open until 11pm in summer) devoted to the work of sculptor and painter Marino Marini (1901–80).

Via della Spada leads back to Via dei Tornabuoni, with its elegant shops. The latter then leads off to the left, to the Piazza Antinori. Dominating the right-hand side of the street here is the facade of **San Gaetano** ⓰ (Sun mornings only), which was built in 1604–48. In many ways it is another version of Santa Trinità; the rhythmic decoration, double pilasters and the generously-proportioned steps make the facade a great deal more monumental, though. The interior, in *pietra serena*, is surprisingly sombre.

Directly opposite is the Early Renaissance **Palazzo Antinori** ⓱ (closed to the public). The wine-growing Antinori family have owned it since 1506.

Via Rondinelli now curves around to join Via dei Cerretani; on the first street to the right is the church of **Santa Maria Maggiore** ⓲ (8am–noon, 4–6pm), a good church on which to practise recognising various different styles. The facade is Romanesque, the portal is 14th-century Gothic; the interior is a combination of baroque exuberance, Renaissance windows and Gothic pointed arches.

Star Attraction
- Palazzo Rucellai

Dye dynasty
The Rucellai were one of the great Florentine families, who formed a marriage alliance with the Medici in 1461. Their family name betrays the source of their wealth: *oricello* was a costly red dye made from a lichen imported from Mallorca.

Below: Palazzo Antinori
Bottom: Marini sculpture

3: Old City Streets

Duomo – Via del Procònsolo – Bargello – Mercato Nuovo – Palazzo Davanzati – Palazzo Strozzi – Orsanmichele – Casa Alighieri – Via del Corso – Duomo

Via del Procònsolo leaves the cathedral square at its southeast corner. On the left, before the intersection with Via del Corso, **Palazzo Nonfinito** ⓳ comes into view. Begun by Buontalenti in 1593, it was continued by Caccini according to designs by Scamozzi, but it remained uncompleted *(nonfinito)*. The gables above the ground-floor windows are a unique feature. Today it houses the Museo Nazionale di Antropologia ed Etnologia.

On the opposite corner is a building attributed to Giuliano da Maiano, the ★ **Palazzo Pazzi** ⓴; built between 1462–72 for Jacopo de' Pazzi. The latter took part in a conspiracy against the Medici in 1478 and was put to death. The facade is very elegant, with rectangular windows on the rusticated ground floor, graceful Rucellai double windows on the first floor, and round Renaissance windows on the second storey.

Art in the Badia

Thanks to the works of art it contains, the interior of the Badia is almost a Renaissance museum: on the left of the entrance is *Madonna Appearing to St Bernard*, by Filippino Lippi (c 1486); on the right is the tomb of Pandolfini, from the workshop of Rossellino (1456), as well as a *Madonna and Saints* and the tombs of Bernardo Giugni and Conte Ugo, by Mino da Fiesole (1469).

Badia Fiorentina entrance

THE BADIA

A short distance further along Via del Procònsolo, two buildings that played important roles in the history of Florence stand opposite one another: the **Badia Fiorentina** ㉑ and the **Bargello** ㉒. The ★ **Badia**, the oldest Benedictine monastery in Florence, was a centre of religious and spiritual power, while the Bargello (1255) became the centre of political and secular authority when the city was run by the *Primo Popolo* (1250–60).

Very little remains of the original structure of the Badia (open Mon only 3–6pm) apart from its outer walls. The building was radically altered in 1627. There is a good view of the ★ **campanile** from the cloister outside the main entrance: the storeys of this hexagonal tower clearly reveal the transition from Romanesque to Gothic. On the right of the main altar a door leads to the charming, two-storeyed ★ **Renaissance cloister**.

THE BARGELLO

The massive, battlemented medieval fortress opposite is the famous ★★ **Bargello** (open daily 8.15am–1.50pm; closed first, third and fifth Sunday and second and fourth Monday of the month), the oldest seat of government in the city. The side facing the street and the tower were built by monk-architects Sisto and Ristoro from Santa Maria Novella (construction work began in 1255), and the rear section was added by Neri di Fioravanti (1332–45). Later, the interior was radically altered (mostly as a result of the building being used as a prison, 16th–18th century).

Since 1865 the Bargello has been a museum, housing an outstanding collection of Florentine Rennaisance sculpture as well as many remarkable *objets d'art*. But just as awe-inspiring as many of the exhibits here is the medieval ★ **inner courtyard**, with its groin-vaulted arcades and 14th-century stone staircase, with the coats-of-arms of the powerful along its walls.

Star Attraction
- the Bargello

Below: room with a view
Bottom: Bargello battlements

INSIDE THE BARGELLO

Ground Floor: 16th-century sculpture by Michelangelo and his Florentine contemporaries, Sansovino, Cellini, Giambologna, Bernini, Ammannati, etc.

First Floor: a fine collection of ivories, from

the Etruscan period to the Rennaisance. In the Cappella del Podestá is a ★ **high lectern**, decorated with intarsia. In the main hall are displayed works by Donatello, including the world-famous ★★ **David and the Lion** symbol of Florence, the *Marzocco*. In the same room are Brunelleschi's and Ghiberti's panels for the Baptistry.

Second Floor: colourful enamelled terracottas of the Della Robbia school; Verrocchio room; small Renaissance bronzes; medal collection; seals, etc.

Below: the Bargello inner courtyard
Bottom: San Firenze sculpture

PIAZZA SAN FIRENZE

Via del Procònsolo opens out into the Piazza San Firenze, a busy intersection of seven streets, dominated by two major edifices. On the left is **San Firenze** ㉓, a huge baroque building, built originally as an oratory for the Florentine Filippo Neri, who was canonised in 1622. Construction work began in the 17th century, and the facade dates from 1772–5. Today the building houses the law courts.

Directly opposite is the ★ **Palazzo Gondi** ㉔, built by Giuliano da Sangallo (1490–1501). The massive rustication here and the huge, mysterious portals contrast with the subtly structured upper storeys – this palazzo is a fine example of Florentine Renaissance style.

LUCKY BOAR

The route along Via del Procònsolo as far as the Piazza San Firenze follows the course of the city's first Roman wall, which originally continued along Via della Condotta all the way to the Piazza Santa Trinità. Via della Condotta leads into the heart of medieval Florence, past Via dei Cerchi with its small, elegant shops, and then across Via dei Calzaiuoli.

The street-name now changes to Via Porta Rossa, which leads on to the **Mercato Nuovo** ㉕ (open daily in the summer, closed Sun and Mon in the winter), where lace, straw-work, leather goods and souvenirs can be bought. At the south-east corner, where Via Calimaruzza branches off towards the Piazza della Signoria, the remains of a Roman city-gate (1st century AD) can be seen in the basement of house No 3 (ask the doorman).

The **loggia**, built on a square groundplan, was constructed between 1547 and 1551 for the sale of silk and gold, and is still used as a market booth today. The bronze boar is famous (the fountain is known familiarly as *Fontana del Porcellino*), and touching its snout is supposed to bring good luck. It is the second copy of the original by Pietro Tacca (c 1612) to have stood here. The original is in the Uffizi. The boar's snout points in the direction of the **Palazzo di Parte Guelfa** ㉖, built as the official residence of the Captains of the Guelf Party in the 14th century. The section with the Gothic windows is the oldest, and the rear part of the building, based on a design by Brunelleschi, was added in the 15th century.

THREE PALAZZI

Further along Via Porta Rossa is the ★**Palazzo Davanzati** ㉗, which is now the **Museo dell' Antica Casa Fiorentina** (currently closed for refurbishment; ground and first floors due to open spring, 2002; call to check on 055-238 8610). It is the best surviving example of a 14th-century medieval nobleman's house in Florence.

The house is built around a central courtyard, which could be cut off from the street in times

Star Attraction

- Donatello's David and the Lion

Hawkers to haggle

On Via Santa Maria, just south of the Mercato Nuovo, African street hawkers sell amazingly convincing copies of designer (Gucci, Prada, etc.) handbags. Make sure you bargain.

Below: lucky touch
Bottom: souvenirs at Mercato Nuovo

Maps on pages 34 & 53

Piazza post
Florence's main post office is under the arcades in Via Pellicceria, the southwest corner of Piazza della Repubblica. On Thursdays there is a flower market in Via Pellicceria.

Below: torch-holder on the Palazzo Strozzi (bottom)

of trouble; it contains the main stairway leading to the landings above. The well in the basement served all five floors of the house: a bucket was drawn up a hidden shaft. The kitchen was under the roof (the warmest place in the house), and various utensils are on display there. The first floor contains a whole series of 14th-century household items; much of the flooring is original.

Opposite the Palazzo Davanzati, between the small Piazza Davanzati and Piazza Strozzi, is the ★ **Palazzo dello Strozzino** ㉘. Begun by Medici architect Michelozzo in 1458, the building was continued by Giuliano da Maiano (1462–5), and bears a clear resemblance to the Palazzo Medici-Riccardi *(see page 67)*.

On the corner, Via degli Anselmi leads across Piazza Strozzi to the ★★ **Palazzo Strozzi** ㉙, built for wealthy patrician Filippo Strozzi (died 1491) and used as a venue for temporary exhibits. Strozzi led the last attempt by the Republican exiles to abolish the Medici principate, and was defeated at the battle of Montemurlo. The facade – a mixture of the rather unfriendly, tiny peepholes of the ground floor of the Palazzo Rucellai and the elegant upper floors of the Palazzo Medici-Riccardi – is by Giuliano da Sangallo, and is crowned by a magnificent projecting cornice. The wrought-iron torch-holders were designed by Benedetto da Maiano.

Via dei Strozzi opens out into the **Piazza della Repubblica**, created after the market quarter and the ghetto were demolished in the 19th century. To the southeast of the square, Via Orsanmichele leads to the **Palazzo dell'Arte della Lana** ㉚; originally the headquarters of the wool merchants' guild, the building dates from 1308 and is now the headquarters of the Dante Society.

Star Attractions
- **Palazzo Strozzi**
- **Orsanmichele**

St Peter at Orsanmichele

ORSANMICHELE

Next door to the palazzo is the tall rectangular church of ★★ **Orsanmichele** ㉛ (open Mon–Fri 9am–noon, 4–6pm, Sat and Sun 9am–1pm, 4–6pm; closed first and last Monday of the month), originally built in 1337 as an open loggia for the sale of grain, and converted into a church in 1367. It was built on the site of the 9th-century San Michele ad Hortum, and the arcades were enclosed by three-light Gothic windows in 1380. Although they were filled in shortly after, their tracery can still be seen. The various guilds were allowed to decorate the canopied niches outside the building, and the ★★ **statues of patron saints** they commissioned are a testimony to the skills of Florentine sculptors over a period of some 200 years:

1 *St John the Baptist* by Ghiberti (1414)
2 *Tabernacle* by Donatello and Michelozzo (1425), *Doubting Thomas* by Verrocchio (c1480)
3 *St Luke* by Giambologna (1562)
4 *St Peter* by Donatello (1413)
5 *St Philip* by Nanni di Banco (1412)
6 *Four Crowned Saints* by Nanni di Banco (1408)
7 *St George* by Donatello (1416)
8 *St Matthew* by Ghiberti (1422)
9 *St Stephen* by Ghiberti (1426)
10 *St Elijah* by Nanni di Banco (1415)
11 *St Mark* by Donatello (1411–13)
12 *St James* by Piero Lamberti (1422)
13 *Madonna of the Rose* (1399)
14 *St John the Evangelist* by Baccio da Montelupo (1515)

ORSANMICHELE NICHE STATUES

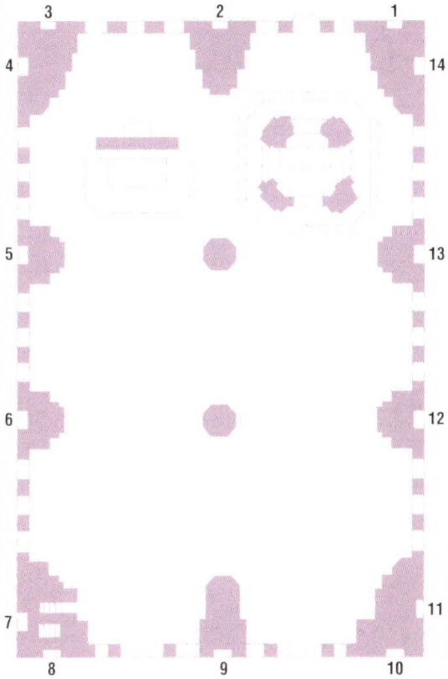

Dante the politician

As well as being a poet, Dante was also an enthusiastic politician. In 1295 he joined the Arte dei Medici e degli Speziali (doctors' and apothecaries' guild), and in 1300 he was elected as one of the *priori* (priors) for two months. He was also a 'White Guelf', rejecting the German emperor but also not wanting to be subjugated by the pope. When the 'Black Guelfs' *(neri)* came to power in 1302, Dante was condemned to death, and went into exile. During the rest of his life he lived in Ravenna – where his grave lies – and also Bologna, Lucca, Verona and Venice.

Casa di Dante

The exterior of the building is decorated with 15th-century enamelled terracotta medallions, bearing the heraldic devices *(stemme)* of the various Florentine guilds, by Luca della Robbia (1399–1482) and his workshop. The interior contains the impressive Gothic ★**tabernacle** by Andrea Orcagna (1355–9), ornamented with marble and coloured glass. The reliefs show *Scenes from the Life of the Virgin*, and the altarpiece has been attributed to Bernardo Daddi. Note too the altar statue of the *Madonna and Child with St Anne* by Francesco da Sangallo (c 1526).

DANTE'S HOUSE

Via dei Tavolini crosses Via dei Cerchi and, after the Piazza de' Cimatori, turns into Via Dante Alighieri; at the junction with Via Santa Margherita stands the **Torre della Castagna**, an ancient 13th-century tower, where the *priori* (priors) used to reside in 1382 before they moved to the Palazzo Vecchio. Opposite is the **Casa di Dante** ㉜ (open Nov–Feb: Wed–Mon 10am–4pm, Sun 10am–2pm; Mar–Oct: 10am–6pm, Sun 10am–2pm), reputedly the home of Dante's parents; the poet Dante Alighieri (1265–1321) probably grew up here. The building is now a museum, with exhibits documenting the life of the poet.

Opposite the house is the small church of **Santa Margherita de' Cerchi** ㉝, Dante's local church, where he probably got married and where he is said to have first caught sight of Beatrice Portinari, whom he idealised in his poetry. The church, which is often used for chamber music and organ recitals, contains a fine altarpiece by Neri di Bicci.

Via Santa Margherita leads through an archway to **Via del Corso**; on the left here is the church of **Santa Margherita in Santa Maria de' Ricci** ㉞, with a porticoed facade dating from 1611. The interior, altered in the 18th century, is a fine example of neoclassicism, with painted ceiling, side altars, pillars and wrought-iron balustrades created by Zanobi del Rosso in 1769.

Via del Corso extends as far as Via de' Calzaiuoli, which then leads back to the Piazza del Duomo.

4: Across the Arno

Ponte Vecchio – Borgo San Jacopo – Ponte Santa Trinità – San Frediano – Brancacci Chapel (Santa Maria del Carmine) – Santo Spirito – Palazzo Pitti – Boboli Gardens – Fortezza di Belvedere – Santa Felicità – Ponte Vecchio

The narrowest part of the Arno, where the ★★ **Ponte Vecchio** (Old Bridge) now stands, formed part of an important trading route to Volterra as far back as Etruscan times. In Roman times the Via Cassia – the road connecting Rome with Florence – crossed the Arno here, and from the Early Middle Ages onwards there were several reports about the bridge being unable to withstand the Arno's floods. After the inundation of 1333, redevelopment work began: to stem the floods, tall walls were built, as was the stone bridge still in existence today (built either by Neri di Fioravanti or Taddeo Gaddi).

★

Star Attraction
- **Ponte Vecchio**

Below and bottom: aspects of Ponte Vecchio

SHOPPING BRIDGE

The south bank of the Arno, the so-called *Oltrarno*, had been settled long beforehand and was enclosed by the third city wall, and so renting out the shops on the bridge was a useful source of extra income for the city-state. The shops were then sold off in around 1600, and this resulted

Bust of Cellini

in the adventurous-looking structures for which the Ponte Vecchio is famous today. In 1565 Vasari built the Corridoio for Cosimo I *(see page 38)*, which crosses the Arno here.

In 1593 the decision was taken to allow only goldsmiths, silversmiths and jewellers to use the shops on the bridge, which until then had been traditionally used by butchers. There is a monument in the middle of the bridge to one of the city's greatest goldsmiths, Benvenuto Cellini, whose *Perseus* can be seen in the Loggia dei Lanzi.

San Jacopo

The **Borgo San Jacopo** runs parallel to the Arno through the quarter of the same name. Its narrow streets and ancient doors, with their charm-

ing terracottas (No 17 has a good *Annunciation*), lend historic atmosphere. The originally Romanesque church of **San Jacopo sopr'Arno** ㉟ (open only for concerts) has a 13th-century portico.

At the end of the Borgo San Jacopo, in front of the **Ponte di Santa Trinità**, is the Piazza Frescobaldi. A striking feature of the facade of the **Palazzo Frescobaldi** ㊱ is the imaginative design of the windows in the centre portal. The building, which dates from the 13th century, was later given baroque additions. At No 1 Lungarno Guicciardini is the **Palazzo Capponi** ㊲; the salon on the first floor was completely covered with allegorical frescoes in honour of the Capponi family by Bernardo Poccetti (1585). The Palazzo Lanfredini (home of the British Institute Harold Acton Library) at No 9 still bears traces of decoration on its 16th-century facade.

After the Ponte alla Carraia, the view across the Arno stretches as far as the green expanse of the Cascine public park. With its main entrance facing the Arno is **San Frediano in Cestello** ㊳ (open Mon–Sat 9.30am–noon and 4.30–6pm, Sun 4.30–6pm only), a bizarre-looking architectural complex consisting of an unfinished facade, a fine dome surmounted by a lantern, and also a playful, slender campanile.

The building (1680–98) is Florentine baroque. The chapels inside are also domed, and were painted by 18th-century masters, as was the huge cupola. The polychromatic marble altar has portals left and right extending up to the side walls. The west end has a fine organ-loft, and the third chapel on the left contains a 13th-century painted wooden statue of the *Smiling Madonna*.

SANTA MARIA DEL CARMINE

To the right of the church, Via di Cestello joins the Borgo San Frediano; follow the latter round to the left, and the first turning to the right leads into the piazza containing the church of **Santa Maria del Carmine** ㊴ (open daily 8–10am and 5–7pm). This building, with its interesting rough stone facade, contains one of the greatest

Demo dome
According to Vasari, the dome of San Jacopo sopr' Arno was a practice-run for Brunelleschi before he went on to do the big one on the Cathedral.

Below: San Frediano in Cestello
Bottom: Santa Maria del Carmine, Brancacci Chapel

…on pages 56 & 59

treasures of Italian painting in its transept, which together with the sacristy survived a fire unscathed in the year 1771.

The ★★★ **Brancacci Chapel** (open Mon and Wed–Sat 10am–5pm, Sun 1–5pm; closed Tues) is easily on a par with Michelangelo's Sistine Chapel in Rome and Giotto's frescoes in the Cappella degli Scrovegni in Padua. The painters commissioned by the Brancacci, a family of wealthy silk merchants, were Masolino da Panicale and Masaccio. Masolino had a style that was still traditionally Gothic, while Masaccio (1401–28) continued Giotto's early realism via the application of the new rules of perspective, and he thus forms the artistic link between Giotto and Michelangelo. His frescoes gain their vivid, animated quality from the clever use of light and shade *(chiaroscuro)* to create depth.

Work on the frescoes was broken off abruptly in 1427 for reasons that are still unknown; the cycle was only completed some 50 years later, after Masaccio's death, by Filippino Lippi (1483).

The Brancacci frescoes include the Temptation of Adam and Eve *(below) and the* Resurrection of the Son of Theophilus *(bottom)*

FRESCOES BY MASOLINO

1 *Temptation of Adam and Eve*
2 (with Masaccio) *The Raising of Tabitha*
3 (with Masaccio) *The Healing of the Cripple*
4 *The Sermon of St Peter*

FRESCOES BY MASACCIO

5 *The Expulsion from Paradise*
6 *The Tribute Money*
7 *The Baptism of the Neophytes*
8 *St Peter Distributing Alms*
9 *St Peter Healing the Sick with his Shadow*
10 *St Peter Enthroned* (the friar with the red hood is thought to be Masaccio himself)

FRESCOES BY FILIPPINO LIPPI

11 *Release of St Peter from Prison*
12 *St Peter Arguing with Simon* (self-portrait of Lippi to the right of the painting)
13 *Crucifixion of St Peter*
14 *Resurrection of the Son of Theophilus*
15 *St Peter in Prison Visited by St Paul*

SANTO SPIRITO

From the church square Via Santa Monaca leads to Via de' Serragli, passing the tiny church of **Santa Monaca** 40, with its charming Renaissance facade. After the intersection the street becomes Via San Agostino, and opens out into the elegant **Piazza Santo Spirito**, a fine leafy square to relax in. There's a flea market here on the second Sunday of the month and an organic produce market every third Sunday.

Towering above the square to the right is the **Palazzo Guadagni** 41, a model 16th-century Florentine mansion, probably built by Cronaca (1503). It has fine graffiti decoration on its facade and a superb top-floor loggia beneath its projecting roof. The loggia belongs to the **Hotel Sorelle Bandini**, a rather faded old pensione; Room 4 has access to the loggia.

The rather modest 18th-century facade of ★★**Santo Spirito** 42 (open daily 8.30am–noon and 4–5.30pm; closed Wed afternoon) can be seen at the top of the piazza. The facade of the church is due to be restored at any time; the work will be sponsored by the Gucci comapny,

Star Attractions
• **Brancacci Chapel**
• **Santo Spirito**

God and Mammon

The content of the Brancacci frescoes is closely associated with the family who commissioned them. The newly wealthy class of merchants had theological problems, because the church was opposed to the idea of anyone earning interest – even though that was the mainstay of the city's prosperity. Bearing this in mind, Masaccio's *Tribute Money* and *St Peter Distributing Alms* almost seem to justify the practice. After all, Christ himself acknowledged the necessity of paying tribute money, and the Brancacci family were distributing their worldly goods too, by commissioning this magnificent chapel for all believers.

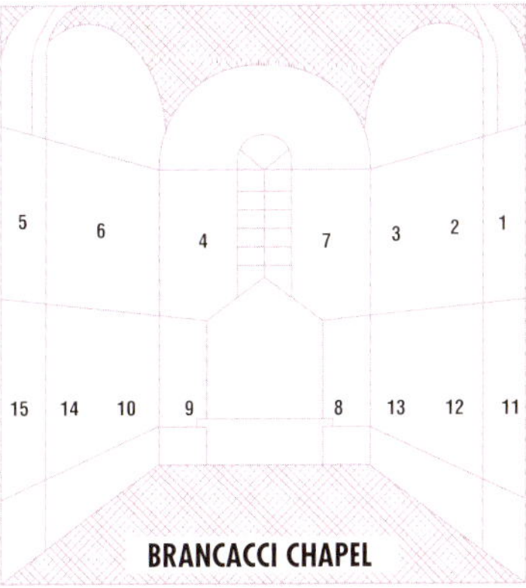

Maps on pages 56 & 61

Misdirected

Brunelleschi's plan was to build Santo Spirito as a counterpart to San Lorenzo *(see page 68)*, so the two churches would face each other from opposite banks of the Arno. After his death the whole edifice was aligned in a different direction – and neither of the churches has ever had its facade completed.

whose headquarters are in the area. The previous building on this site was destroyed by fire in the 13th century, and in 1444 Brunelleschi was commissioned to design a new church for the Augustinians. But he died two years later, and in 1487 his design was finally realised – not too successfully – by Antonio Manetti, Giovanni da Gaiole and Salvi d'Andrea. Salvi built the dome as he thought fit and missed out the facade entirely; the slender campanile is a contribution by Baccio D'Agnolo (1503–17).

INSIDE SANTO SPIRITO

The interior of Santo Spirito reveals Brunelleschi's sure command of form, witnessed by the feeling of order and harmony, the austere use of colour, and the perspective of the colonnades and vaulted aisles. The master architect replaced the walls with a continuous series of 40 chapels around the entire church, anticipating the baroque style in his search for the mastery of space.

The many paintings inside this church provide a glimpse into the work of several of the less well-known masters of the Renaissance; the gradual transition in the backgrounds from smooth gold to perspective landscape appears here in many variations. Here is a selection of the finer pieces *(see plan on page 61)*.

Below: S. Spirito stained glass
Bottom: view along the nave

1 *Madonna and Child with the Young St John, Saints and Donors* by Filippino Lippi (1490)
2 Marble sarcophagus of Neri Capponi by Bernardo Rossellino (1457)
3 *Madonna and Saints* by Lorenzo di Credi (early 16th-century)
4 *Annunciation*, Florentine school (15th-century)
5 *Nativity*, Domenico Ghirlandaio school (15th-century)
6 *Madonna with Child, Angels and Saints*, attributed to Francesco Granacci (15th-century)
7 *Santa Monica Founding the Order of Augustinian Nuns* by Francesco Botticini (15th-century)
8 *Madonna with Child and Saints* by Cosimo Rosselli (15th-century)
9 Marble altar by Andrea Sansovino (1492) in the shape of a triumphal arch
10 *Trinity* attributed to Raffaellino del Garbo (1470–1525)
11 *Madonna with Angels, St Bartholomew, St Nicholas of Bari and Two Donors* by Raffaellino del Garbo
12 *Madonna with Child and Four Saints* by Raffaellino del Garbo
13 Vestibule by Andrea Sansovino
14 Sacristy by Giuliano da Sangallo and Cronaca (1489): domed octagon and double pilasters in Florentine Renaissance style

Madonna and Child with the Young St John

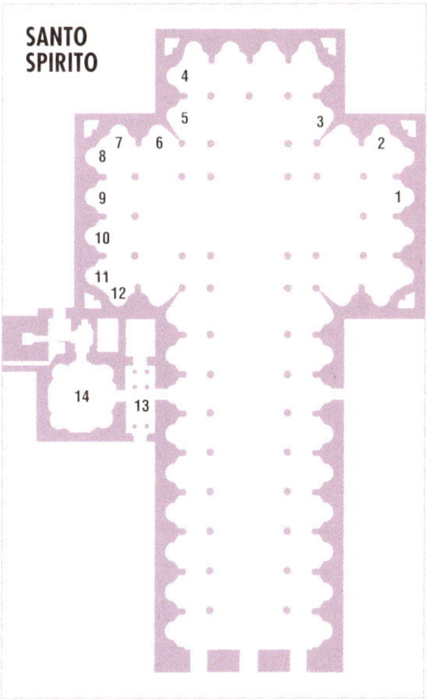

THE REFECTORY

To the left of the church is the entrance to the ★ **Cenacolo di Santo Spirito** (open Tues–Sat 9am–1.30pm, Sun 8am–12.30pm; closed Mon), the former refectory, now a museum. On the rear wall is a magnificent *Crucifixion* fresco, and also a *Last Supper*, both attributed to Andrea Orcagna (c 1360). The sculptures on display here are rare architectural and decorative fragments from the Romanesque and pre-Romanesque periods.

Map on page 56

'MAIN STREET'

Next to the facade, Via de' Michelozzi branches off to join with Via Maggio. In the past this was probably called 'Maggiore' – main street – because of its sharp contrast with the tiny medieval alleys around it. It used to be the main traffic artery leading across the Arno to the city centre, and was used for processions, tournaments and games. A stroll along here today is definitely worthwhile if only to admire the many elegant antique shops. The facade of No 26, the **Palazzo di Bianca Cappello** (43), should certainly not be missed either. It was designed by Buontalenti (c 1570), and was once the home of famous courtesan Bianca Cappello, the mistress (and then wife) of Francesco I, Duke of Florence (1541–87). The graffiti decoration is by Poccetti (1548–1612).

Below and bottom: aspects of Palazzo Pitti

THE PITTI PALACE

After its junction with Via Maggio, Via de' Michelozzi becomes the Sdrucciolo de' Pitti, a quiet little street at the end of which the immense ★★ **Palazzo Pitti** (44), with its 205-metre (670-ft) wide facade, suddenly comes into view. The Pitti were rivals of the Medici, and commissioned Brunelleschi to design the main section of the palace around the year 1440. Told to outdo all the other palazzi in Florence, he came up with seven

bays, with three doorways and four windows on the ground floor, and seven windows on the upper ones. The Medici responded with the ten-bay Palazzo Medici-Riccardi *(see page 67)*. The Pitti family's fortunes then waned, and they were forced to stop building in 1470, finally even having to sell the palazzo in 1549 to Eleonora of Toledo, wife of Cosimo I.

The building was immediately extended, with a feeling for style that was rare for that time: the same materials and forms used in the central section designed by Brunelleschi were simply enlarged. This was done by Ammannati in 1560, by Giulio and Alfonso Parigi in the 17th century, and by Giuseppe Ruggieri in the 18th, resulting in the building's present-day appearance. It looks far more forbidding than the palazzi of the Medici, Rucellai and Strozzi in the city centre, firstly because of its location on a rise, and secondly because the upper floors lack the usual double windows and finer structuring, and thus do not alleviate the heavy rustication at ground level.

GALLERY OF MASTERPIECES

The Palazzo Pitti today contains museums with first-class exhibits, and is itself a museum, documenting as it does four centuries of magnificent interior design. The entrance is on the right-hand side of the inner courtyard; a grand staircase leads up to the museum floors.

The ★★ **Galleria Palatina** (open Tues–Sun 8.15am–6.50pm) takes up the entire left-hand side of the palace. Before being converted into galleries, these rooms were magnificent palace apartments, and so worth visiting for the interior decoration alone, which was executed in the high baroque style by Pietro da Cortona (1596–1669). It served as a model for many European palaces.

The art gallery, with its works by many of the world's most famous painters, adds an extra aesthetic dimension to the place, though for many it can seem too much of a good thing: the paintings have been hung simply with an eye to decoration, with no connection in content or

★

Star Attractions
- Palazzo Pitti
- Galleria Palatina

Changing rooms
The route you follow to view the works in the Galleria Palatina is subject to change, depending on the restoration work being carried out at any given time, and some rooms may be unexpectedly closed.

Raphael's Maddalena Doni

Map on page 56

otherwise, nor any relation to the rooms or the decoration around them.

The Galleria Palatina contains masterpieces by Titian, Giorgione, Raphael, Rubens, Van Dyck, Rosso Fiorentino, Murillo, Fra Bartolomeo, Andrea del Sarto, Velázquez, Caravaggio, Allori, Filippino Lippi, Luca Signorelli, Guido Reni, Paolo Veronese and Antonio Canova.

STATE ROOMS

A ticket to the Galleria Palatina also gives you entrance to the **Appartamenti Monumentali** (State Apartments), on the right-hand side of the ground floor. Four centuries of courtly life can be observed here: in the 16th century the Medici moved into this 15th-century Early Renaissance building and decorated it in accordance with contemporary taste. Later, in the 18th century, the Austrian grand dukes resided here until Italian unification in 1860. The last potentates to live here were the kings of Italy up until World War I.

Another series of rooms on the ground floor, lavishly decorated on the occasion of the grand marriage of Ferdinando II in 1634, today form the **Museo degli Argenti** (Silver Museum; open daily 8.15am–6.30pm; closed second and fourth Sunday and first, third and fifth Monday of the month). The 17th-century frescoes here glorify

'Modern' art

On the second floor of the Palazzo Pitti, modern paintings are on display in the Galleria d'Arte Moderna (Gallery of Modern Art), but since this gallery was founded in 1860, 'modern' actually means late 18th- and 19th-century works (sculptures, paintings, arts and crafts).

The Boboli Gardens

the Medici family. The exhibits include priceless works of art made with precious stones, ivory and metals from the treasury of Ferdinando III and of the prince-bishops of Salzburg.

Star Attraction
- **Boboli Gardens**

BOBOLI GARDENS

On the hillside behind the palace lie the magnificent ★★ **Boboli Gardens** (Giardino di Boboli; open Nov–Feb 9am–4.30pm; Mar 9am–5.30pm; Apr, May, Sept and Oct 9am–6.30pm; June–Aug: 9am–7.30pm; closed first and last Monday of the month). They were laid out on the order of Eleonora of Toledo by Ammannati, then by Buontalenti and Alfonso Parigi. Constituting the biggest public park in the centre of Florence, these gardens, with their charming fountains, are among the finest in Italy.

It is best to enter from the north wing of the palace, where the path follows the final stretch of the corridor from the Pitti to the Palazzo Vecchio. Beneath its walls is the so-called Fontana del Bacco (Bacchus Fountain), actually a statue of the pot-bellied court dwarf of Cosimo I, and a little further on is the Grotta del Buontalenti, an imaginative and artistic grotto created in the Mannerist style by Buontalenti (1583–8), with casts of Michelangelo's *Slaves*, frescoes by Poccetti and statues by Bandinelli. *Paris and Helen* (by Vincenzo de' Rossi, 1560) face one another in the second cave, while *Venus* (by Giambologna, 1573) can be seen emerging from her bath in the third one.

Below: the Bacchus Fountain
Bottom: the Neptune Fountain

AMPHITHEATRE

The path now winds uphill, passing the **Anfiteatro** (Amphitheatre) laid out like a Roman circus and decorated with antique statues (or copies). The view gives an idea of just how majestic the setting once used to be for performances staged in the palace courtyard. The path leads on up to the Neptune Fountain; the bronze statue of the sea-god is by Stoldo Lorenzi (1565). At the top is a colossal statue of *Abundance* by Giambologna, completed by Pietro Tacca (1636).

Map on page 56

Security conscious
Originally there was only one entrance to the Fortezza di Belvedere – a secret door entered from the Boboli Gardens behind the Pitti Palace. Even today, access is so limited that when exhibitions are held here, the larger sculptures have to be lifted in by helicopter.

Modern sculpture at the Fortezza di Belvedere

The path left leads to the rococo Kaffeehaus (open in the summer only), left here by the Austrians in 1776, with its terrace and stunning views of the centre of Florence. Above it loom the imposing walls of the **Fortezza di Belvedere** ㊺, which the Medici had built between 1590 and 1595, not to enjoy the magnificent panorama it affords, but to fire on the city in the event of uprisings. This fortified villa was designed by Buontalenti, and today is used for exhibitions.

SANTA FELICITA

Leaving the Fortezza, keep to the left, staying within the fortifications, and then stroll downhill along the Costa San Giorgio. This is a quiet part of the city, with the odd fine view. You eventually emerge at the ancient church of **Santa Felìcita** ㊻ (open Mon–Sat 9am–noon, 3–6pm, Sun 9am–1pm), which stands on the site of an Early Christian cemetery. The church underwent alterations in the 11th and 14th centuries, before it was given its present-day appearance in the 18th century by Ferdinando Ruggieri (1736).

The Corridoio Vasariano *(see page 38)* goes past this church and thus had to be built into it. The Medici could participate in the services held here via the golden grille on the rear wall. Ruggieri built a single-aisled interior with a barrel vault, trapezoid windows and projecting balconies, with a repeated 'grille' motif – possibly in anticipation of neoclassicism.

In the Cappella Capponi, which was designed by Brunelleschi in 1425 in his favourite centralised manner, there is a fine Mannerist *Deposition* by Pontormo (1538), who also painted the *Annunciation* fresco in the dome; three of the Evangelists in the tondi of the cupola are also by him, and the fourth (with the angel) is by Agnolo Bronzino. The sacristy contains a polyptych of the *Madonna and Child with Saints* by Taddeo Gaddi (14th-century), and also *St Felicity and her Seven Sons* by Neri di Bicci (15th-century). On the parvis, some fragments of Palaeochristian tomb inscriptions are on display (4th to 5th-century).

5: San Lorenzo and Santa Maria

Duomo – Palazzo Medici-Riccardi – San Lorenzo – Santa Maria Novella – Ognissanti – Lungarno Corsini – Ponte Vecchio

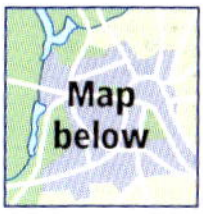

Next to the Baptistry, Via de' Martelli leaves the Piazza del Duomo and heads north. At No 22r along this busy street is the Libreria Marzocco, one of the best bookshops in the city. At the first intersection, the ★★ **Palazzo Medici-Riccardi** ㊼ (entrance in the inner courtyard) comes into view.

This building was the seat of the Medici (their coat-of-arms can still be seen halfway up the wall on the corner) until they moved into the Palazzo Vecchio in 1540. Cosimo the Elder asked Michelozzo to build the palazzo in 1444, and he designed a square building in accordance with

Star Attraction
- **Palazzo Medici-Riccardi**

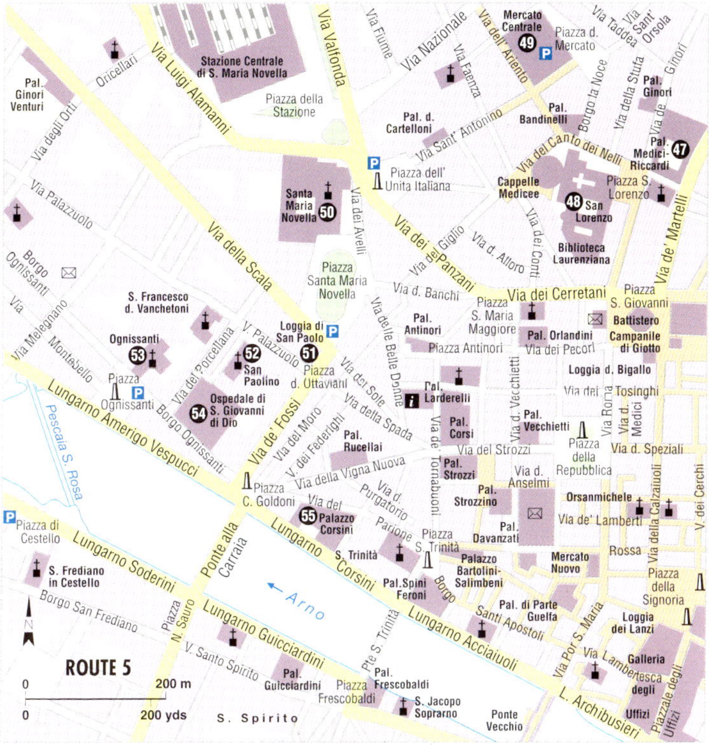

Maps on pages 67 & 71

Closely guarded
Don't be surprised if you see swarms of police outside the Palazzo Medici-Riccardi: the building now houses Florence's prefecture, and they are stationed there to guard visiting VIPs.

contemporary taste for rustification. The original sides were the length of the facade, with its 10 bays along Via de' Gori; the Riccardi family later enlarged the building by adding a further seven bays along Via Cavour (1684–9).

The rustication on the ground floor is 8m (26ft) high, and has round arches set into it. The ones on the corners were open, and Michelangelo filled them with playful windows in 1517. The upper storeys have double-windows, and the rustication higher up is altogether more gentle. The cornice, modelled on Antiquity, completes the structure.

CAPPELLA DEI MAGI

The Riccardi family's alterations to the palace left only one 15th-century jewel behind: Michelozzo's ★★ **Cappella dei Magi** on the first floor (open Thur–Tues 9am–7pm). The well-restored decorative frescoes (1459–60) showing the *Procession of the Magi to Bethlehem* are the masterpiece of Benozzo Gozzoli, and they depict many contemporary personalities, including the Medici family – young Lorenzo the Magnificent on the white horse, his father Piero di Cosimo behind him wearing a red beret, and the latter's brother Giovanni.

This seemingly endless triumphal procession across a Tuscan landscape is closely associated with political events of the time: all forces were then being mobilised to recapture Constantinople, which had fallen to the Turks in 1453.

Sculpture at the Palazzo Medici-Riccardi

SAN LORENZO

The tiny Via de' Gori leads along the battlemented garden wall of the Palazzo Medici to the Piazza San Lorenzo, filled with a busy street market selling clothing and souvenirs. The line of houses here follows the route taken by the second city wall. The seated statue (1540) of Giovanni delle Bande Nere is by Baccio Bandinelli.

The most distinctive feature here, though, is the archaic-looking, incomplete facade of ★★ **San Lorenzo** ㊽ (open Mon–Sat 10am–5pm), which was consecrated by St Ambrose, Bishop of Milan, in the year 393. The present structure was commissioned by the Medici from 1420, according to designs by Brunelleschi. After the latter's death, his work was continued by Antonio Manetti (1447–69) and then by Michelangelo (c 1520–34), who rounded off the whole project by adding not just two sacristies but also the Medici Chapels and the Biblioteca Medicea-Laurenziana. In 1740 the campanile was added by Ferdinando Ruggieri.

Star Attractions
- **Capella dei Magi**
- **San Lorenzo**

INTERIOR

It was inside San Lorenzo that Brunelleschi first presented the formal language he had derived from Florentine Romanesque *(see page 18)*. To achieve a rational spatial clarity he used round arches, pillars, capitals, pilasters, entablature and round windows.

1 Interior facade designed by Michelangelo (c 1518)
2 *Marriage of the Virgin* by Rosso Fiorentino (1494–1540); Gothic tomb-slab of the organist Francesco Landini (died 1397)
3 Tabernacle by Desiderio da Settignano, prototype in central perspective (1461)
4 Main altar in polychrome marble (1787); crucifix by Baccio da Montelupo (16th-century)

Below: the nave of San Lorenzo
Bottom: the cloisters

Maps on pages 67 & 71

5 Memorial slab to Cosimo the Elder by Verrocchio; Donatello's sarcophagus below

6 *Madonna* in polychrome wood (14th-century)

7 *Annunciation* by Filippo Lippi (1406–69)

8 *Martyrdom of St Lawrence* fresco by Bronzino (1503–72)

9/10 ★★ **Pulpits** by Donatello (c 1460) and his workshop, with bronze relief of the Passion. Brunelleschi created the cube-shaped ★★ **Old Sacristy** with its hemispherical dome, and Donatello was responsible for the sculpture (medallions, altar, portals, statues)

11 Marble sarcophagus of Cosimo the Elder's parents, by Cavalcanti (1433)

12 Sarcophagus of Giovanni and Piero de' Medici by Verrocchio (1469–72), from porphyry, bronze, marble and serpentine

13 Little chapel with lavabo by the Verrocchio school. The cloister then leads to the ★ **Biblioteca Medicea-Laurenziana** (open Mon–Fri 9am–1pm)

14 Library vestibule, with the surprising solution Michelangelo chose for the staircase (1524–6)

15 Reading Room: walls, floor, ceiling and inlaid desks all designed by Michelangelo (begun in 1524, consecrated in 1571)

16 Sarcophagus of Giuliano de' Medici with

Artist's sketches
Within Michelangelo's New Sacristy, some of his architectural drawings for column bases can be seen on the walls on either side of the altar. In the little room to the left of the altar, charcoal sketches also attributed to Michelangelo were discovered in 1975. This room is not open to all, but a limited number of visitors are admitted between 9am and noon. Ask at the ticket office.

Dramatic fresco in the dome

Michelangelo's allegorical figures *Day* and *Night*

17 Sarcophagus of Lorenzo de' Medici, with the reclining allegorical figures of *Dawn* and *Dusk*. Lorenzo appears as a Thinker

18 Architectural monument to Lorenzo the Magnificent and his brother Giuliano. The work is incomplete; the *Madonna and Child* are by Michelangelo, while the statues of St Cosmas and St Damian are by Montorsoli and Raffaello da Montelupo (1533)

Star Attractions
- Donatello's pulpits
- Old Sacristy
- New Sacristy
- Medici Chapels

San Lorenzo's dome

MEDICI CHAPELS

These last three are in the ★★ **New Sacristy**, attached to the south transept. This was Michelangelo's first architectural commission, and while he employed the same basic centralised structure of Brunelleschi's Old Sacristy, he also rendered it with sculptural additions that endow this family chapel with a magnificent grandeur. Double pilasters accentuate the idealised statues of the city's rulers.

The entrance to the ★★ **Cappelle Medicee** (Medici Chapels; open Tues–Sat 8.30am–5pm; first, third and fourth Sun, and second and fourth Mon 8.30am–1.30pm) is outside the church, in the Piazza della Madonna degli Aldobrandini.

It was Grand Duke Cosimo I who first insisted on a further mausoleum for the Medici family. The ★ **Cappella dei Principi** was designed by his illegitimate son, Don Giovanni de' Medici, then begun by Matteo Nigetti in 1604. Work continued until as late as 1836. This imposing-looking octagonal structure with its dome contains some incomparably fine *pietra-dura* (decorative stone-work).

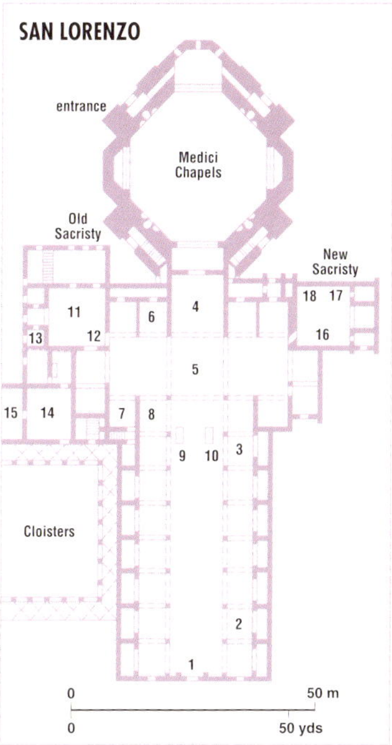

CENTRAL MARKET

Via dell'Ariento, packed with market stalls like the rest of this area, branches off towards the **Mercato Centrale** ㊾,

Map on page 67

Mercato Centrale
The ground floor of the covered Mercato Centrale is a great place to buy picnic food: cheeses, meats and pâtés. The fruit and vegetables are upstairs.

Below: Mercato Centrale roof
Bottom: the facade of Santa Maria Novella

the central food market (open Mon–Sat 7am–1pm); to the left, the narrow Via Sant'Antonio leads off to the Piazza dell'Unità Italiana, where there is a view of the modern station of Santa Maria Novella.

SANTA MARIA NOVELLA

★★ **Santa Maria Novella** ㊿ (open Mon–Sat 9.30am–5pm, Fri and Sun 1pm–5pm) is the most important Gothic church in Tuscany. A mendicant order basilica like Santa Croce *(see page 90)*, it was built outside the city walls. The facade and the parvis can be reached by walking around the cemetery. There are two obelisks on the parvis: Cosimo I was fond of horse-racing and had them placed there as turning markers.

EXTERIOR

Construction work on the present-day version of the church (a building on this site is first mentioned in the 10th century) began in 1246. The Dominicans, who were given the property, chose the simple, unadorned style favoured by mendicant orders – no grandeur, functional architecture, and simple rectangles instead of polygonal variety. The facade was begun in 1300, but remained unfinished until the rich patrician Giovanni Rucellai came up with the funds to have it completed. He commissioned architect Leon Battista Alberti in 1458 – on condition that he retained the already completed lower part of the facade and the large round window.

The tiny dichromatic Gothic niches with two narrow doors can be seen in the lowest section. Alberti accentuated this section by adding a powerful main portal with pillars. Its entablature, combined with the pillars on the outside of the facade, gives the ground floor an entirely new look. Alberti placed the round window at the centre of an eye-catching mezzanine with square patterns. As for the problem of connecting the lower floor and the gable on the facade, Alberti made a historic decision and chose scrolls – a solution that was imitated on facades everywhere.

Interior

The raised section of the floor from the seventh bay onwards is a reminder that the friars' choir began there, before it fell victim to Vasari's 'modernisation' between 1565 and 1572, along with the rood screen. This church contains some very valuable works of art, for the mendicant orders allowed wealthy families to use chapels – and those families spared no expense in decorating them. The Rucellai managed to have their family emblem (a billowing ship's sail) included alongside that of the Medici (a ring with ostrich feathers) in a magnificent inlaid frieze along the entire length of the facade.

Star Attraction
• Santa Maria Novella

Below: detail of a fresco by Ghirlandaio in Santa Maria
Bottom: facade detail

Santa Maria's Art

The *Nativity* above the portal on the inside has been attributed to Fra Filippo Lippi (15th-century); the *Coronation of the Virgin* at the rose window is by Andrea da Firenze (c 1365); in the second side-altar on the right is the tomb of Beata Villana by Bernardo Rossellino and workshop (1451). Next to the fifth pillar on the right is the entrance to the Cappella della Pura (1474), containing a 14th-century Madonna that supposedly has miraculous powers.

Stairs in the right transept lead down to the Cappella Rucellai (14th-century), containing the

bronze tomb-slab of Lionardo Dati by Ghiberti. The Cappella Strozzi (on the right of the main altar) contains frescoes by Filippo Lippi (1497–1502): in the vault are *Adam, Noah, Abraham and Jacob*; on the right-hand wall is the *Martyrdom of St John the Evangelist*; and behind the altar is the elaborately carved tomb of Filippo Strozzi by Benedetto da Maiano (1491–3).

At the main altar is a bronze crucifix by Giambologna (14th-century) and superb frescoes by Domenico Ghirlandaio (1485–90). In the Cappella Gondi, to the left of the main altar, is a wooden crucifix by Brunelleschi, his only sculpture to survive in wood, carved some time between 1410 and 1425.

Below: lavabo by della Robbia
Bottom: stained glass and frescoes

NORTH TRANSEPT

A flight of steps in the left transept leads to the Cappella Strozzi di Mantova, containing frescoes of *The Last Judgement*, *Hell* and *Paradise* (based on Dante's *Divine Comedy*) by Nardo di Cione (1357). In the sacristy (access via the left transept), the crucifix is an early work by Giotto (before 1300) and the lavabo in terracotta with landscape is by Giovanni della Robbia (1498).

On the way back to the main portal, admire the pulpit (second to last pillar, on the left): it was designed by no less a person than Brunelleschi,

in 1443, and the reliefs show *Scenes from the Life of the Virgin*.

Behind the pillar, in the third side-altar from the end, there is an epoch-making fresco: Masaccio's ★★★ ***Trinity***, which he painted just before his death (1428). Here, Brunelleschi's architectural aesthetic has been rendered in paint: this was the first time since Antiquity that a painter had ever used perspective.

★

Star Attraction

• Masaccio's Trinity

Object lesson

Brunelleschi's wooden crucifix in the Capella Gondi is traditionally thought to have been carved to show Donatello how the Redeemer should be represented. Brunelleschi is said to have called Donatello's crucifix in Santa Croce 'a mere peasant on the cross'.

CLOISTERS

On the left-hand side of the church facade is the entrance to the cloisters, which today are the ★ **Museo di Santa Maria Novella** (open Sat–Thur 9am–2pm). The Chiostro Verde (Green Cloister), so named because of the predominant colour of the frescoes painted here by Paolo Uccello and his workshop (14th-century) on the theme of *Genesis*, was badly damaged in the floods of 1966. At least Uccello's *Diluvio Universale* was saved from destruction. What remained can be admired in the refectory, where Uccello's *Sacrifice of Noah* is also on display (turn left at the end of the cloister).

The entrance to the newly restored **Cappellone degli Spagnuoli** (Spanish Chapel) is marked by sturdy Gothic columns. Originally the Dominican friars' chapter-house, this chapel was built between 1348 and 1355, and the paintings were completed in 1365 by the otherwise little-known artist Andrea da Firenze (died 1377, sometimes also called Andrea di Bonaiuto), who was influenced by the Sienese school of painting.

In 1348, the population of Florence was reduced from 100,000 to just 40,000 by the Black Death. The huge gap in art history after Giotto died in 1337 was a direct result of the plague, as was the yearning for security and order so clearly expressed in these frescoes.

The wall on the right shows the *Church Militant and Triumphant* (the Florence Cathedral depicted here was never built) and the glorification of the actions of the Dominicans. In the foreground, behind a group of kneeling pilgrims, are

Cloister arches

Map on page 67

Dog Latin
Andrea da Firenze's depiction of the Dominicans as dogs in the Spanish Chapel is not disrespectful. The order derives its name from *Domini canes* ('Dogs of the Lord') – an apt name for the friars who saw their role as defending the faithful flock against heresy.

Ognissanti facade

the presumed portraits of Cimabue, Giotto, Boccaccio, Dante and Petrarch; the flock of the faithful is watched over by the Dominican friars, symbolised by dogs attacking heretical wolves.

The opposite wall shows the *Triumph of Divine Wisdom* and the *Glorification of St Thomas Aquinas*; facing the entrance is the *Ascent to Calvary*, the *Crucifixion* and the *Descent into Limbo*; on the vault, the *Resurrection*.

SAN PAULINO

Opposite the church, on the piazza, is the **Loggia di San Paolo** (51), the former entrance to the Spedale San Paolo dei Convalescenti, a kind of parallel institution to Brunelleschi's Ospedale degli Innocenti.

The route now leads through an atmospheric part of Florence that is relatively free of tourists. Turn off Via dei Fossi, lined with antique and artisanal shops, down Via Palazzuolo, with its piazza and the church of **San Paolino** (52). This building, which looks rather odd from the outside, is even more surprising inside (its present form dates from 1669–93). The unadorned interior with its apse, transept, dome and central nave has a connecting balustrade running all the way round that almost seems to be holding everything together.

OGNISSANTI

Via San Paolino passes the right-hand side of the church and then turns right into Via della Porcellana, finally emerging into the Borgo Ognissanti. The church of ★ **Ognissanti** (53) (open daily 8am–12.30pm, 5–7.30pm) is just a few steps away. Its harmonious facade by Matteo Nigetti (1638) contains both Renaissance and baroque elements. The relief of the *Coronation of the Virgin* above the portal is a product of the della Robbia school (c 1515).

Inside, the second altar on the left contains the tomb of the Vespucci family, adorned by a *Madonna della Misericordia* fresco by Ghirlandaio. On the same side is Botticelli's *St Augus-*

tine (1480) and opposite, another Ghirlandaio, this time of *St Hieronymus* (1480). Sandro Botticelli (died 1510) is buried in the family tomb in the last chapel on the right. The refectory in the cloister contains a ★ ***Last Supper*** by Ghirlandaio (1480). The delightful background includes Christian symbols of plants and birds. (Viewing Mon, Tues and Sat only, 9am–noon.)

Piazza Ognissanti contains a 20th-century version of Hercules fighting the Lion. The view from here across to the other bank and the massive San Frediano should not be missed. The Borgo Ognissanti is where Florence originally began to prosper, because from the 11th century onwards Benedictine monks ran cloth- and wool-manufacturing enterprises in this part of the city. Today, the many tasteful and elegant shops make a stroll back through this quarter a real pleasure. At No 26 there is a fine Italian Art Nouveau house, and No 20, the **Ospedale di San Giovanni di Dio** (54), has a superb early 18th-century baroque staircase.

From the Piazza Goldoni the route continues along the bank of the river via the **Lungarno Corsini** as far as the huge **Palazzo Corsini** (55), built in grandiose Roman baroque style (mid 17th-century). The facade is crowned by statues and has a terrace overlooking the river.

The route ends a little further along the Arno at the **Ponte Vecchio**.

Below: detail of Ghirlandaio's Last Supper
Bottom: Palazzo Corsini

6: North of the Duomo

Duomo – Galleria dell'Accademia – San Marco – Giardino dei Semplici (Orto Botanico) – SS Annunziata – Spedale degli Innocenti – Museo Archeologico – Santa Maria de' Pazzi – Sant' Ambrogio – Loggia del Pesce – Duomo

Via Ricasoli leads north from the **Duomo**, passing the Teatro Niccolini on the way, and, just before the junction with Via degli Alfani, the mighty **Palazzo Gerini** ㊻, with its nine-bay facade, appears. The portals on the ground floor flank seven windows with triangular gables, and the nine round windows on the first floor, reinforced with rustication, complete the facade (by Baccio d'Agnolo, 16th-century). The fact that the rustication has 'moved up' from the ground to the first floor shows that it was used purely decoratively rather than for any functional purpose.

Installing *David*
Michelangelo's *David* used to stand in front of the Palazzo Vecchio *(see page 34)* but was replaced by a copy in 1910. Installing the work in 1501 was a massive task: archways were torn down, narrow streets were widened, and it took 40 men five days to move the huge sculpture from the artist's workshop behind the Duomo to the Piazza della Signoria.

'Hard Stone' Workshop

In Via degli Alfani, next door to the Luigi Cherubini Conservatory, is the entrance to the restoration workshops of **Opificio delle Pietre Dure** ㊼ (usually open Mon–Sat 8.15am–2pm, Tues until 7pm). Established in 1580 under Francesco I de' Medici, the workshops developed techniques of producing mosaic pictures using *pietre dure* (literally 'hard stones'). The mosaics were used in wall panels and tabletops, as well as more luxury items. There are exhibits of mosaics on display, and on the upper floor the workshops and tools once used by the craftsmen can be admired.

Opificio delle Pietre Dure entrance

Galleria dell'Accademia

One of the city's main museums is the ★ **Galleria dell'Accademia** ㊽ (open Tues–Sun 8.15am–6.50pm), which contains important collections of sculpture and paintings. Michelangelo's *Slaves*, his *Pietà* and his world-famous ★★★ ***David*** are just three of the main attractions here. The *Slaves* (1519, unfinished), originally destined for the tomb of Pope Julius II, evokes his belief that the sculpture already exists within the block of stone and the sculptor's job is merely to release it by removing what is superfluous. The *Pietà* from Palestrina near Rome is not now thought to be by Michelangelo, but his colossal statue of *David* established him as the foremost sculptor of his time at the age of 26.

Star Attraction
- **Michelangelo's David**

Michelangelo's David

PICTURES AND VIOLINS

The Accademia also has a picture gallery, containing many fine examples of 14th- and 15th-century Tuscan painting (Paolo Uccello, Orcagna, Taddeo Gaddi, Botticelli, etc) as well as work by 16th-century Tuscan Mannerists (Pontormo, Allori, Bronzino). There is a fine collection of musical instruments housed in a ground floor room at the Accademia, which includes instruments by Stradivarius, Guarneri and others.

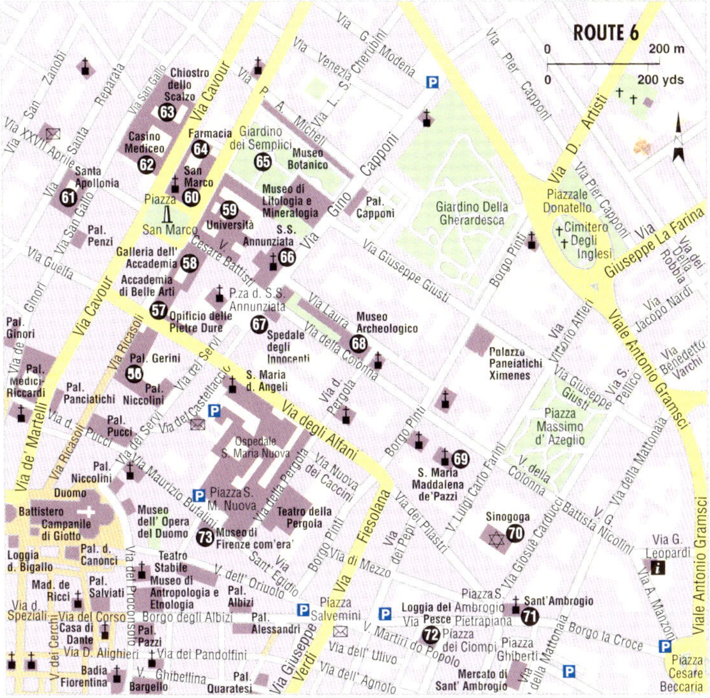

Maps on pages 79 & 81

Below: San Marco facade
Bottom: inside the church

SAN MARCO

Via Ricasoli emerges into the Piazza San Marco, where the **University** (59) is situated. This part of the city is always full of students. **San Marco** (60), with its church, monastery and museum (open daily 7am–noon, 4–8pm), is a favourite with art-lovers, though the church is the least interesting bit: despite dating back to 1299, it suffered from alterations during the 17th and 18th centuries and received a neoclassical facade in 1780. Worthy of note inside the church are a crucifix in the style of Giotto (14th-century), the *Baldachin Madonna* by Fra Bartolomeo on the second altar on the right (1509), and at the next altar the *Madonna in Prayer*, an 8th-century Roman mosaic (705–7).

MONASTERY AND MUSEUM

The Cappella di Sant'Antonino contains the tomb of St Antonino of Florence (1389–1459), who as archbishop was responsible for the construction of the **monastery** next door. Cosimo the Elder (a rich banker) paid for the monastery, and Michelozzo built it between 1437 and 1452. The new occupants were Dominican monks from Fiesole, and their disciplined, ascetic lifestyle is reflected in the architecture.

Michelozzo's building, the first Renaissance monastery, is sober and severe in contrast to the

formal exuberance of his contemporary Brunelleschi: discipline and asceticism forbade pure decoration. An austere form of architecture thus developed which eschewed anything superficial – just the right environment for the paintings by the artist-monk Fra Beato Angelico. San Marco is virtually his museum.

The entrance to the ★★ **Museo di San Marco** (open Mon–Fri 8.15am–1.50pm, Sat 8.15am–6.50pm, Sun 8.15am–7pm; closed first, third and fifth Sunday and second and fourth Monday of the month) is next to the church.

Star Attraction

• **Museo di San Marco**

'Blessed Angel'

Fra Beato Angelico (his real name was Guido di Pietro) entered the Dominican convent in Fiesole at the age of 20, where he worked initially as an illustrator of manuscripts. He came down to Florence when his order took over San Marco, and for nine years produced frescoes for the new building – his most famous works. In the last decade of his life, Angelico also worked in Orvieto, Perugia and Rome, where he died in 1455.

GROUND FLOOR

1 Entrance from the piazza, and vestibule

2 Cloister of St Antonino, by Michelozzo; the lunettes with scenes from the life of the saint were added much later and detract from the originally very austere and meditative effect

3 Above the church door, Fra Angelico's lunette of *St Peter Martyr* enjoining silence

4 *St Dominic at the Foot of the Cross* (Fra Angelico)

5 Sala del Capitolo (Chapter House). *St Dominic with the Rule of the Order*; for discipline to be maintained, monks had to accept punishment here. *Crucifixion and Saints*; Christ as Redeemer (Fra Angelico)

6 Sala del Lavabo (Lavatorium). Above the door, an exquisite *Pietà* by Fra Angelico; *Madonna with St Anne and Saints* (Fra Bartolomeo)

7 Refettorio Grande (Refectory). Frescoes from the Fra Bartolomeo school

8 Above the door to the Hospice: *Christ as a Pilgrim* (Fra Angelico)

9 Ospizio dei Pellegrini. Exhibition of tablets by Fra Angelico; on the front wall one of his main works *The Descent from the Cross* (1435)

10 Above the door *Thomas Aquinas* (Fra Angelico)

11 Chiostro di San Domenico by

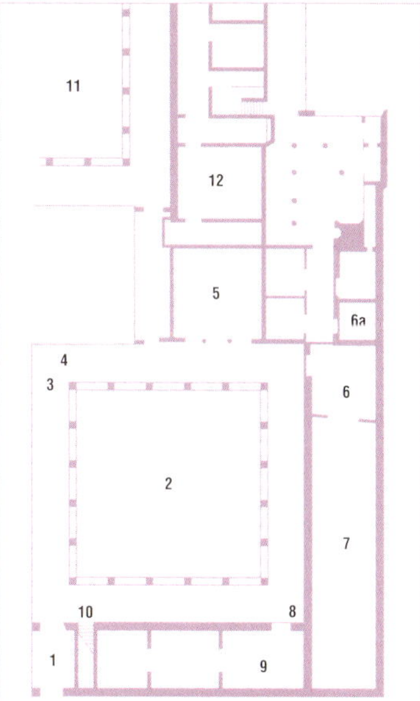

MUSEO SAN MARCO
GROUND FLOOR

Maps on pages 79, 81 & 82

Savonarola

Girolamo Savonarola was Prior of San Marco from 1491 to 1498 – a tumultuous time during which the French King Charles VIII invaded Italy and drove the Medici from Florence. Savonarola presided over the new republic for four years, and with evangelical fervour urged the Florentines to abandon their paintings, sculptures and luxuries in favour of a higher spirituality. He had both fanatical supporters and equally determined opponents. Popular opinion finally turned against him in 1498 and he was executed.

Michelozzo; the arcades contain material salvaged after the demolition of the Ghetto and the Mercato Vecchio in the 19th century to make way for the Piazza della Repubblica

12 Refettorio Piccolo (Small Refectory). *The Last Supper* by Ghirlandaio (1480–90)

13 *The Last Judgement* by Fra Bartolomeo

FIRST FLOOR

The Dormitory beneath the huge wooden roof consists of 44 small monastic cells, each with their own vault and adorned with an intimate fresco (by Fra Angelico and his assistants c 1438–45). The following is a selection.

1 *Jesus Appears to Mary*

2 *The Annunciation* (c 1445; one of Fra Angelico's most famous works)

3 *Transfiguration*

4 *Coronation of the Virgin*

5 Prior's room, where Savonarola also lived; his portrait by his supporter Fra Bartolomeo

6 Savonarola's cell

7 Savonarola's sleeping chamber; the banner he carried when preaching

8 Cell of St Antonino

9 Cell of Fra Angelico

10 *Prayer on the Mount of Olives with Madonna and St Martha*

11 *Communion of the Apostles*

12/13 Cosimo the Elder retired to these cells

14 The first public library of the Renaissance, by Michelozzo.

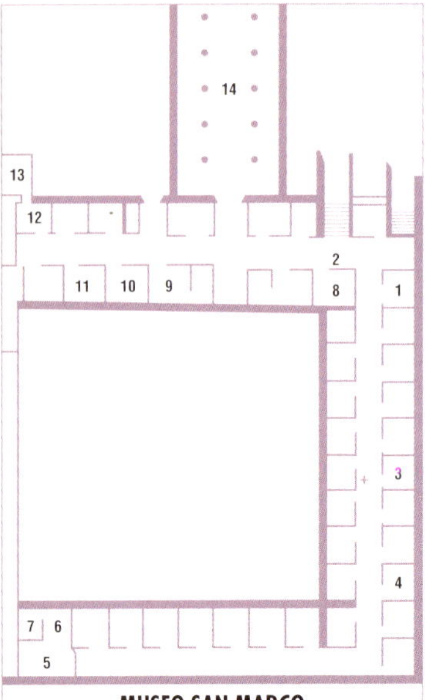

MUSEO SAN MARCO
FIRST FLOOR

SANT'APOLLONIA

From the Piazza San Marco, Via XXVII Aprile leads to the former convent of ★**Sant' Apollonia** ❻❶ (open daily 8.15am–1.50pm; closed first, third and fifth Sunday and second and fourth Monday of the month), where the ★★ ***Last Supper*** fresco by Andrea del Castagno (1445–50) can be admired in the refectory. Once concealed under whitewash, it now reveals the influence of Masaccio's pictorial illusionism and Castagno's use of perspective.

On Via Cavour, which runs past the church of San Marco, Nos 55, 57 and 59 are all taken up by an impressive building, the **Casino Mediceo** ❻❷. The 11-bay facade was devised by Bernardo Buontalenti (1536–1608).

At No 69 in the same street is the modest entrance to the **Chiostro dello Scalzo** ❻❸ (open Mon–Thur 9am–1pm). Andrea del Sarto (1468–1530) painted a cycle of monochrome frescoes in stages here on the *Life of St John the Baptist* and *Allegories of the Virtues* (two panels have been attributed to his workshop).

The ★ **Farmacia** ❻❹ over the road at No 146r is also a rewarding place to visit: it has a magnificent painted ceiling and some fine glazed terracotta decoration.

BOTANICAL GARDEN

Anyone keen on taking a break at this point will find Florence's botanical garden, the **Giardino dei Semplici** ❻❺ (open Mon and Fri 9am–noon, 2.30–5pm, Wed 9am–noon), around the next corner, just a few steps away from the pharmacy. It was laid out by order of Cosimo I in 1545.

Via Giorgio La Pira, on which the Giardino dei

★

Star Attraction

- **Castagno's Last Supper**

Below: pot plants in the Giardino dei Semplici
Bottom: at the entrance of the Chiostro dello Scalzo

Semplici lies, comes out into the Piazza San Marco, where a left turn down Via Cesare Battisti leads to the most beautiful square in Florence. ★ **Piazza della Santissima Annunziata**, designed by Brunelleschi, is surrounded on three sides by porticoes. The equestrian statue of Grand Duke Ferdinand I was designed by Giambologna and executed in 1608 by Pietro Tacca, who also contributed the two ★ **fountains** (1629).

Below and bottom: Santissima Annunziata, atrium details

SANTISSIMA ANNUNZIATA

Behind the portico of the church of **Santissima Annunziata** ⓺⓺ (open daily 8am–noon, 4–6pm; closed Wed afternoon) lies an atrium with frescoes showing *Scenes from the Life of the Virgin*, and also early works by Andrea del Sarto (*Birth* and *Arrival of the Three Magi*, the latter with the artist's self-portrait in the right-hand corner).

The atrium was designed by Michelozzo, who rebuilt the entire complex in 1444. It was the only part of the building to survive the later structural changes. The addition of a **gilt ceiling** (1669) and baroque decoration during the centuries that followed simply interfered with the original architectural clarity. The rotunda was completed in the year 1477.

Here is a selection of the **works of art** within the church. Left of the entrance is a large circular tribune (designed by Michelozzo, 1461) with a fresco of the *Coronation of the Virgin* in the cupola. The fresco of *St Julian and the Saviour* in the first chapel on the left, and the fresco of the *Trinity* in the second chapel to the left are both by Andrea del Castagno (c 1455). The Chiostro dei Morti (Cloister of the Dead) is entered from the door in the north transept: the fresco of ★ ***Madonna del Sacco*** (the Madonna with the Sack), the most famous work by Andrea del Sarto (1525), is over the door. At the end of the cloister on the left is the Cappella di San Luca, or 'Artists' Chapel', which has belonged to the Accademia delle Arti del Disegno since 1565. Many famous artists lie buried here, including Pontormo (1567) and Benvenuto Cellini.

SPEDALE DEGLI INNOCENTI

Begun in 1421, Filippo Brunelleschi's ★★ **Foundling Hospital** (Spedale degli Innocenti) 67 (open Thur–Tues 8.30am–1.30pm) is the very first building in Renaissance form. Commissioned by the Arte della Seta (silk guild), Brunelleschi employed a variety of proto-Renaissance motifs to create a formal language for the Early Renaissance. His facade here consists of a colonnade on the ground floor with slender Corinthian columns and wide semicircular arches, and a first floor with generously spaced rectangular windows under shallow pediments. Medallions in coloured terracotta by Andrea della Robbia – the famous babes in swaddling clothes sold in cheap copies by the souvenir-dealers in Florence – are placed into the spandrels of the arcade.

The art gallery in the Foundling Hospital contains a fine *Coronation of the Virgin* by Nero di Bicci (15th-century) and also the magnificent ★*Adoration of the Magi* by Ghirlandaio (1488).

ARCHAEOLOGICAL MUSEUM

Spread out along Via della Colonna is the ★**Museo Archeologico** 68 (open Mon 2–7pm, Tues and Thur 8.30am–7pm, Wed and Fri–Sun 8.30am–2pm). The collections here focus on Greek–Roman Antiquity, ancient Egypt and also

Star Attraction
- Foundling Hospital

First orphanage
The Spedale degli Innocenti, opened in 1445, was Europe's first orphanage – and part of the building is still used for this purpose. In its early years, mothers could leave unwanted babies here anonymously by placing them in a revolving stone cylinder, or *rota*, on the left of the portico, and ringing the bell. The stone was then turned and the child taken in.

The Foundling Hospital

Map on page 79

the Etruscans. There are some important bronzes, particularly the Etruscan ones on the first floor. The famous 5th-century Chimera, part lion, part snake and part goat, is here. In the same corridor is the Orator from the Hellenistic period, and a statue of Minerva.

Below and bottom: Museo Archeologico exhibits

SANTA MARIA MADDALENA

At No 58 Borgo Pinti, the second street to intersect Via della Colonna after the museum, an inconspicuous-looking door leads the way to one of the most magnificent frescoes in the whole city, in the convent of ★ **Santa Maria Maddalena de' Pazzi** ❻❾ (open daily 9am–noon and 5–7pm).

An atrium lined with pillars leads into the church itself, which dates back to 1257. It is a fine example of Florentine baroque, restored after the floods of 1966. The trapezoid windows are a typical feature, as is the presbytery, completed in 1685. The golden and reddish tones of the main altar stand out against the dark marble floor. Cupola frescoes (Piero Dandini) and paintings with *Scenes from the Life of the Virgin* (Luca Giordano) complete the harmonious scene.

On the right before the presbytery, signposted passageways lead to the former chapter house, which contains a ★★ **fresco** of the *Crucifixion* by Perugino. The clarity and magnificence of the

fresco (1493–5) are immediately striking: the ample sculpturesque figures are gracefully posed; the harmonious space is tightly controlled in the foreground and middle ground, while the background gives the impression of infinite space.

Star Attraction
- **Perugino's Crucifixion**

'FLORENCE AS IT WAS'

From the Borgo Pinti, the route continues down Via dei Pilastri, a small street with lots of little shops. Via Luigi Carlo Farini joins this street from the left, and contains the **Synagogue** (Tempio Israelitico) ❼⓿ (open Sun–Thur 10am–3pm, Fri 10am–2pm), built in the Spanish-Moorish style between 1874 and 1882. Its tall green dome and wealth of decoration make it somewhat reminiscent of a mosque.

Via dei Pilastri leads directly to the piazza and the church of **Sant'Ambrogio** (71) (open daily 8am– noon, 4–6pm), one of the oldest churches in Florence, containing the tombs of sculptors Mino da Fiesole (1430–84) and Andrea Verrocchio (1435–88). The left-hand side-chapel contains a marble *Tabernacle* by Mino, with terracotta angels from the Della Robbia school; the church's historic facade can be seen on a processional fresco dating from 1486.

Via Pietrapiana now heads straight back towards the city centre, past the **Loggia del Pesce** (72), now reconstructed on this spot. Vasari built it as a fish market in 1567, but it had to make way for the Piazza della Repubblica in the 19th century. Beyond the loggia there is now a very lively and pretty ★ **Mercato delle Pulci** (flea market, open Mon–Fri), with permanent stalls where all sorts of bargains can still be found.

The continuation of Via Pietrapiana towards the city centre is Via dell'Oriuolo, which passes the museum called **Firenze com'era** ('Florence as it once was') (73) (open Fri–Wed 9am–2pm). This former convent houses an interesting collection of pictures, engravings and drawings of Florence from medieval times to the present. Via dell'Oriuolo then emerges back at the starting point of the route, the Piazza del Duomo.

Lively market
South of Sant'Ambrogio, in Piazza Ghiberti, is the **Mercato di Sant'Ambrogio**, the city's second-largest produce market (the biggest is the Mercato Centrale – *see page 71*), housed in a rather deteriorating cast-iron market hall, and a wonderfully lively place to shop in the company of the locals.

Flea market wares

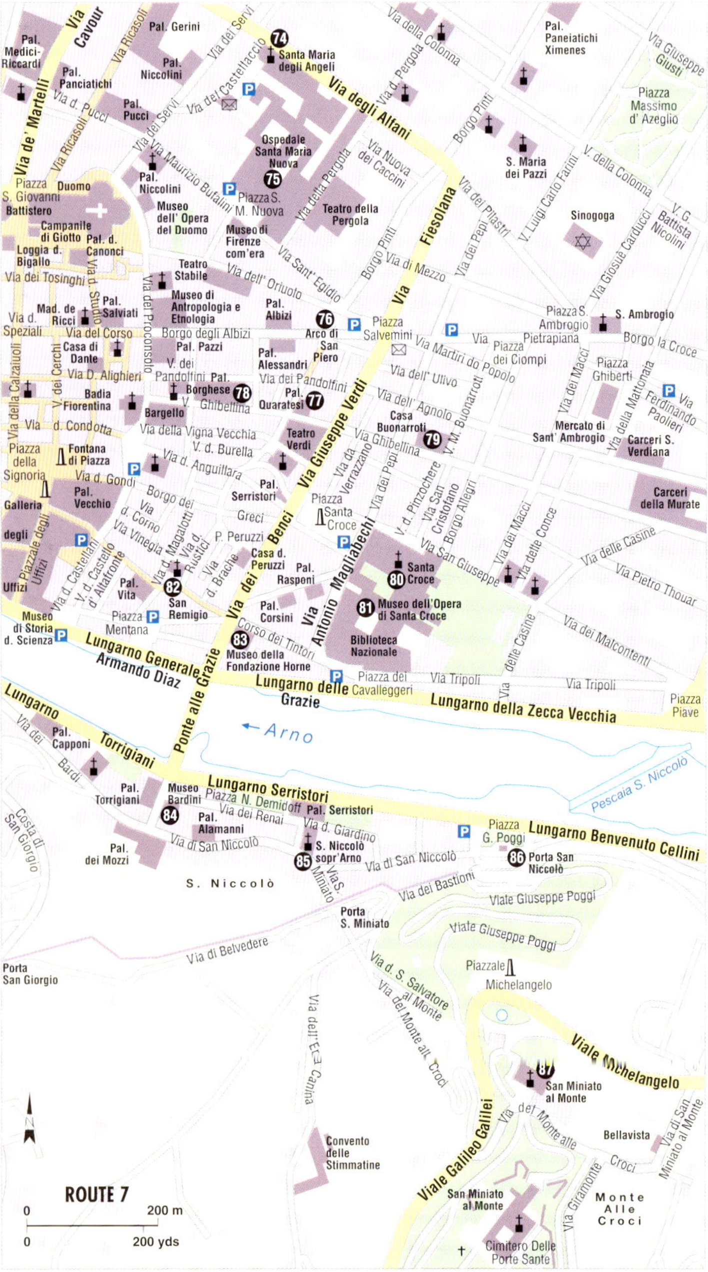
Pal. Medici-Riccardi
Via Cavour
Pal. Gerini
Via Ricasoli
Via dei Servi
74
Santa Maria degli Angeli
Pal. Niccolini
Pal. Panciatichi
Via d. Pucci
Pal. Pucci
Via del Castellaccio
P
Via degli Alfani
Via d. Pergola
Via della Colonna
Pal. Paneiatichi Ximenes
Via Giuseppe Giusti
Piazza Massimo d' Azeglio
Via de' Martelli
Via Ricasoli
Via dei Servi
Ospedale Santa Maria Nuova
75
Via Maurizio Bufalini
Pal. Niccolini
Piazza S. Giovanni
Duomo
Battistero
Campanile di Giotto
Pal. d. Canonci
Loggia d. Bigallo
Museo dell' Opera del Duomo
Piazza S. M. Nuova
Museo di Firenze com'era
Via della Pergola
Teatro della Pergola
Via Nuova dei Caccini
Borgo Pinti
Via Fiesolana
Via dei Pilastri
S. Maria dei Pazzi
V. Luigi Carlo Farini
V. della Colonna
Sinogoga
V. G. Battista Nicolini
Via Giosuè Carducci
Via dei Tosinghi
Via d. Studio
Via del Proconsolo
Teatro Stabile
Via dell' Oriuolo
Via Sant' Egidio
Borgo Pinti
Via di Mezzo
Via dei Pepi
Mad. de Ricci
Pal. Salviati
Museo di Antropologia e Etnologia
Pal. Albizi
76
Arco di San Piero
Piazza Salvemini
Via Martiri do Popolo
Piazza S. Ambrogio
S. Ambrogio
Borgo la Croce
Via d. Speziali
Via del Corso
Borgo degli Albizi
Casa di Dante
Pal. Pazzi
V. dei Pandolfini
Pal. Alessandri
Via dei Pandolfini
Via Pietrapiana
Piazza dei Ciompi
Via dell' Ulivo
Via dei Macci
Piazza Ghiberti
Via Ferdinando Paolieri
Via della Calzaiuoli
V. dei Cerchi
Via D. Alighieri
Pal. Borghese
78
Ghibellina
Pal. Quaratesi
77
Via Giuseppe Verdi
Via dell' Agnolo
Casa Buonarroti
79
V. M. Buonarroti
Mercato di Sant' Ambrogio
Via della Mattonaia
Carceri S. Verdiana
Badia Fiorentina
Via d. Condotta
Bargello
Via della Vigna Vecchia
V. d. Burella
Teatro Verdi
Via Ghibellina
Via da Verrazzano
Piazza della Signoria
Fontana di Piazza
Via d. Anguillara
Via d. Gondi
Pal. Vecchio
Pal. Serristori
Piazza Santa Croce
Via dei Pepi
V. d. Pinzochere
Via San Cristofano
Borgo Allegri
Carceri della Murate
Galleria degli Uffizi
Borgo dei Greci
Via d. Corno
Via Vinegia
Via d. Magalotti
Via d. Rustici
P. Peruzzi
Via dei Benci
Via Antonio Magliabechi
Via dei Macci
Via delle Conce
Via delle Casine
Piazzale degli Uffizi
Via d. Castellani
V. d. Castello d' Altafronte
Pal. Vita
82
San Remigio
Via d. Brache
Casa d. Peruzzi
Pal. Rasponi
Santa Croce
80
Via San Giuseppe
Via Pietro Thouar
Museo di Storia d. Scienza
Piazza Mentana
Pal. Corsini
81
Museo dell'Opera di Santa Croce
Via dei Malcontenti
Lungarno Generale Armando Diaz
83
Corso dei Tintori
Museo della Fondazione Horne
Biblioteca Nazionale
Via delle Casine
Ponte alle Grazie
Lungarno delle Grazie
Piazza dei Cavalleggeri
Via Tripoli
Lungarno della Zecca Vecchia
Piazza Piave
Lungarno Torrigiani
Via dei Bardi
Pal. Capponi
Arno
Pescaia S. Niccolò
Pal. Torrigiani
Museo Bardini
84
Lungarno Serristori
Piazza N. Demidoff
Pal. Serristori
Via dei Renai
Pal. Alamanni
Via d. Giardino
Piazza G. Poggi
Lungarno Benvenuto Cellini
Costa di San Giorgio
Pal. dei Mozzi
Via di San Niccolò
S. Niccolò sopr'Arno
85
Via S. Miniato
86
Porta San Niccolò
S. Niccolò
Via dei Bastioni
Viale Giuseppe Poggi
Porta S. Miniato
Via di Belvedere
Porta San Giorgio
Via d. S. Salvatore al Monte
Via del Monte alle Croci
Piazzale Michelangelo
Via dell'Erta Canina
Viale Michelangelo
87
San Miniato al Monte
Via del Monte alle Croci
Bellavista
Via di San Miniato al Monte
Viale Galileo Galilei
Convento delle Stimmatine
Via Giramonte
Monte Alle Croci
San Miniato al Monte
Cimitero Delle Porte Sante
ROUTE 7
0
200 m
0
200 yds

7: Santa Croce and San Miniato

Map on page 88

Duomo – Santa Maria degli Angeli – Santa Maria Nuova – Arco San Piero – Via Ghibellina – Casa Buonarotti – Santa Croce – Ponte alle Grazie – Porta San Niccolò – Piazzale Michelangelo – San Miniato al Monte

Via dei Servi leaves the Piazza del Duomo on the northeastern side of the cathedral (opposite the left transept), and at its junction with Via dei Pucci the Medici coat-of-arms can be seen, with its seven balls. The next turning to the right, Via del Castellaccio, opens out into the Piazza Brunelleschi, with the octagonal church of **Santa Maria degli Angeli** (Rotonda Brunelleschi) **74**.

Via degli Alfani intersects with Via della Pergola, which contains the theatre of the same name. Via della Pergola then joins Via Sant'Egidio, and from here **Santa Maria Nuova** **75**, the oldest hospital in the city, with its 17th-century arcades and busts of the Medici, is just a few steps away. It was founded in 1286.

At the other end of Via Sant'Egidio is a small square with an arched entrance, the **Arco di San Piero** **76**, beyond which there is a fine view over the city's towers and rooftops. A small vegetable market and several shops and restaurants cater to the needs of this very lively quarter. The narrow, pedestrianised **Borgo degli Albizi** is a good place for a stroll.

Unfinished first

After returning from Rome in 1433, Brunelleschi designed Santa Maria degli Angeli as the first centralised structure of the Renaissance, but it was never completed. Today it is used as a language laboratory by the university.

Below: San Miniato facade
Bottom: Casa Buonarroti bust

MICHELANGELO'S HOUSE

At the second crossroads, Via Matteo Palmieri joins **Via Ghibellina**; to the left on the corner is the 14th-century **Palazzo Quaratesi** **77**, and a few metres further on to the right is the **Palazzo Borghese** **78**. This gigantic neoclassical building has no less than 21 bays – a Florentine record. The projecting central section is adorned by two symmetrical wings.

In the opposite direction on the left is the ⋆ **Casa Buonarroti** **79** (open daily except Tues 9.30am–2pm). Buonarroti was Michelangelo's family name, although the artist never actually

Maps on pages 88 & 91

lived here. He bought the house for a nephew and the family lived here until their line died out in 1858. Today it is a museum. In the vestibule to the right of the entrance hall is a fine bronze *Head of Michelangelo* by Daniele da Volterra. The room to the left at the top of the stairs contains two early works by Michelangelo: the *Madonna of the Steps*, a marble bas-relief, supposedly his first ever sculpture, and *Battle of the Centaurs* (1492), carved just before the death of Lorenzo the Magnificent, and left unfinished.

Stendhal syndrome
The beauty of Santa Croce, in particular the Capella Niccolini, sent Stendhal's head reeling in 1817. The French writer described feeling dizzy and 'in constant fear of falling to the ground' – the first documented case of 'Stendhal syndrome'. Today Florence's hospitals actually record about a dozen cases a year of sensory overload resulting from too much art, too much beauty, simply too much Florence.

SANTA CROCE

Via delle Pinzochere leads to the colonnade on the northern side of ★★ **Santa Croce** **80**, Florence's Franciscan church (open summer Mon– Sat: 9.30am–5.30pm, Sun 3–5.30pm; winter: Mon–Sat 8am–12.30pm, 3–5.30pm, Sun 3–5.30pm). The present building was begun in 1294 by Arnolfo di Cambio, and construction work continued until 1442. The facade and the campanile date from the 19th century, and their ornate marble contrasts with the simple brickwork of the original structure.

The bright, 115-m (380-ft) long interior is lined by solemn arcades of pointed arches, and has an open timber roof. The main altar is emphasised by the polygonal apse and the stained-glass

Door detail, Santa Croce

windows. The wealth of art treasures in this church and its sheer architectural magnificence make Santa Croce one of the most popular sights in Florence, and it was chosen as a last resting place by many of the city's inhabitants. The floor alone has 276 tomb-slabs, and there are tombs of many famous people in the aisles.

Star Attraction
- **Santa Croce**

Cenotaph to Dante in Santa Croce

RIGHT-HAND SIDE-AISLE

1 *Madonna del Latte* by Antonio Rossellino (1427–70)
2 Tomb of Michelangelo by Vasari (1564)
3 Cenotaph to Dante by Stefano Ricci (1829). Dante is buried in Ravenna
4 Tomb of the poet Vittorio Alfieri by Canova (1810)
5 Tomb of Niccolò Machiavelli (1469–1527) by Innocenzo Spinazzi (1787)
6 *Annunciation*, Donatello's masterpiece in gilded limestone. To the left is the tomb of humanist Leonardo Bruni (1369–1444), an influential Renaissance funerary monument by Bernardo Rossellino
7 Tomb of the composer Gioacchino Rossini (1792–1868) by Giuseppe Cassioli (1886); left of the altar is the tomb of poet Ugo Foscolo (1939)
8 Cappella Castellani with fresco cycle by Agnolo Gaddi (c 1383)
9 Cappella Baroncelli. The *Madonna and Child* in the lunette on the Baroncelli tomb has been attributed to Giotto's pupil Taddeo Gaddi (father of Agnolo) who also did the four *prophets* above it and the *Scenes from the Life of the Virgin* (1332–8) on the walls; on the right wall is the *Madonna of the Girdle* by Bastiano Mainardi (late 15th-century); the altarpiece, *Coronation of the Virgin*, is by Giotto and workshop
10 Sacristy Corridor by Michelozzo, with Gothic windows
11 Sacristy (14th-century), containing

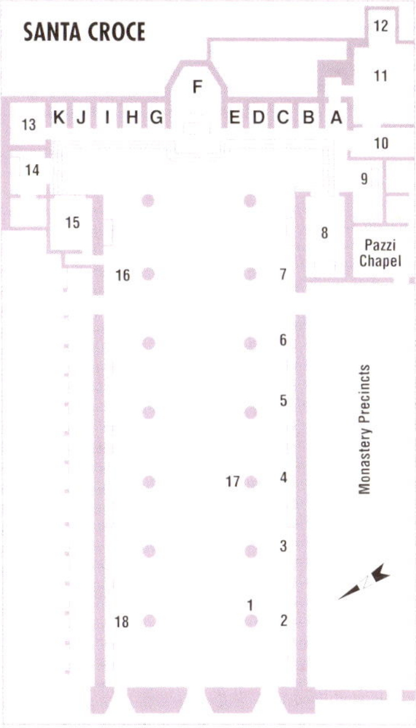

Maps on pages 88 & 91

Below: Santa Croce's choir
Bottom: Giotto's Life of St Francis

fresco of the *Passion* by Niccolò Gerini (c 1380); intarsia furniture by Giovanni di Michele (c 1454); *Crucifixion* by Taddeo Gaddi (14th-century)

12 Cappella Rinuccini with Gothic wrought-iron grille (1371) and frescoes showing *Scenes from the Life of the Virgin and St Mary Magdalen* by Giovanni da Milano and workshop; polyptych by Giovanni del Biondo (1379)

CHOIR CHAPELS

Florentine families filled the chapels on either side of the main altar with works of art.

A Cappella Velluti, with damaged frescoes of the *Archangel Michael*, possibly by Cimabue

B Cappella Calderini, rebuilt by Gherardo Silvani (c 1640); damaged vault painting by Giovanni di San Giovanni (1621)

C Cappella Bonaparte (Giugni) with tombs of the Bonaparte family (19th-century)

D Cappella Peruzzi with ★★ **frescoes** by Giotto in his mature period (c 1320): on the left, *Scenes from the Life of John the Baptist*, and on the right, *Scenes from the Life of St John the Evangelist*

E Cappella Bardi with more ★★ **frescoes** by Giotto (c 1317) including *The Life of St Francis*; ★ **Altarpiece** of St Francis and 20 *Scenes*

from his Life by Barone Berlinghieri (13th-century)

F Cappella Maggiore (sanctuary) with frescoes by Agnolo Gaddi (c 1380): *Legend of the Cross*; polyptych of *Madonna and Saints* by Niccolò Gerini and workshop; crucifix by the 'Master of Figline'; stained-glass lancet windows by Agnolo Gaddi

G Cappella Tosinghi e Spinelli with an *Assumption of the Virgin* by the 'Master of Figline'; altarpiece by Giovanni del Biondo (1372)

H Cappella della Madre Italiana, dedicated to the mothers of those who died in World War I (Libero Andreotti, 1926)

I Cappella Ricasoli, with *St Antonio of Padua* by Luigi Sabatelli and workshop (1840)

J Cappella Pulci with frescoes by Bernardo Daddi (c 1330): *Martyrdom of St Lawrence and St Stephen*; terracotta altar by Giovanni della Robbia (early 16th-century)

K Cappella Bardi di Vernio with frescoes by Maso di Banco (c 1340): *Life of St Sylvester*; altarpiece by Giovanni del Biondo; in the niches, a *Last Judgement* attributed to Maso di Banco and a *Deposition* attributed to Taddeo Gaddi (14th-century)

LEFT-HAND SIDE-AISLE

13 Cappella Niccolini, designed by Giovanni Antonio Dosio (1579–85), with paintings by Alessandro Allori (1588)

14 Cappella Bardi containing a wooden crucifix by Donatello (c 1425)

15 Cappella Salviati with the *Martyrdom of St Lawrence* by Jacopo Ligozzi (c 1600); to the left of the entrance is the tomb (1869) of composer Luigi Cherubini (1760–1842)

16 Tomb of Carlo Marsuppini (1398–1453) by Desiderio da Settignano, who drew inspiration from Rossellino's Bruni tomb opposite

17 Pulpit by Benedetto da Maiano (1472–76) with delicately carved *Scenes from the Life of St Francis*

18 Tomb (1737) of Galileo Galilei (1574–1642)

Star Attraction
- **Giotto frescoes**

Galileo's tomb
Condemned by the church in 1616 for his revolutionary ideas of the earth's place in the solar system, Galileo Galilei was denied a Christian burial until 1737, when the tomb by Giulio Foggini was erected in Santa Croce.

The tomb of Galileo

Map on page 88

Pazzi conspiracy
Andrea Pazzi, head of a wealthy banking family in the Santa Croce neighbourhood, was the man who commissioned Brunelleschi to design a family chapel. Unfortunately for him, he was also the most prominent member of the 'Pazzi conspiracy', a failed attempt to overthrow the Medici in 1478. Giuliano de' Medici was killed but his brother Lorenzo survived. Andrea was executed and the rest of the Pazzi family banished.

PAZZI CHAPEL

Before leaving the church, take a look at the rose window in the west front with its *Deposition* by Giovanni del Ponte (15th-century). In front of the church, turn left and enter the **cloister**: its harmonious arches betray the identity of its designer – Brunelleschi. At the end of it is one of his greatest works, even though he never completed it: the ★★ **Pazzi Chapel** (open Thur–Tues 10am–12.30pm and 2.30–6.30pm). It was begun in 1443, finished in 1461, 15 years after Brunelleschi's death, and is a masterpiece of the Florentine Renaissance.

A hemispherical dome covers a central square, extended on either side so that it forms the centre of a rectangle. Opening off the main square is a corresponding square apse covered by a dome and containing the altar. The frieze above the capitals is adorned with angel heads by Desiderio da Settignano. The creamy wall surface is marked off in geometric patterns by dark grey stone. The 12 seated apostles, in polychrome enamelled terracotta, are from the della Robbia workshop. The polychrome roundels of the Evangelists who look down on them may be by Donatello.

SANTA CROCE MUSEUM

Directly opposite, in the refectory, is the **Museo dell'Opera di Santa Croce** ⑧① (open 1 Mar– 31

The Santa Croce cloister, by Brunelleschi

Oct: Thur–Tues 10am–7pm; until 6pm in winter). Among the museum's exhibits is the world-famous ★★★ ***Crucifix*** by Cimabue, which has now been restored after it was almost completely destroyed in the 1966 flood. The fresco on the end wall is by Taddeo Gaddi, and includes *The Tree of The Cross* and a *Last Supper*. Donatello's colossal bronze of *St Louis* is also here, as is Orcagna's *Triumph of Death*.

Star Attraction
- **Cimabue's Crucifix**

PIAZZA SANTA CROCE

The **Piazza Santa Croce** used to be a popular venue for public gatherings and tournaments; it was also where the historic football match called the *calcio* was played – and lost by the German occupiers – during the Carnival of 1530. Today, the statue of Dante (1865) has had to be shifted from the centre to the side of the piazza to make way for the annual *calcio* in costume *(see page 113* for details).

The south side of Piazza Santa Croce has some interesting *sporti* – those projecting upper floors that are so characteristic of Florence. In 1619 the **Palazzo dell' Antella** (No 22) was provided with its colourful decoration in just 20 days by a team of 12 artists under the direction of Giovanni di San Giovanni.

Below: sculpture in Santa Croce
Bottom: Piazza Santa Croce facades

TOWER HOUSE

The end of the square opposite the church is where Via Torta (Crooked Street) begins. The route follows Via dell'Isola delle Stinche (with the best ice cream shop in Florence) and Via dei Bentaccordi as far as the Piazza dei Peruzzi, then goes past some of the oldest buildings in the city and on to Via de' Benci.

This last street has to be followed around to the right, and just after it starts to widen, the mighty 13th-century **Casa-Torre Alberti**, a typical old Florentine family tower, can be seen on the left. This tower belonged to the family of architect Leon Battista Alberti. Its attractive loggia was added in the early 15th century.

Map on page 88

Crowded view

Piazzale Michelangelo, with its famous view over the city, was in danger of being obliterated by the number of coaches that parked there while their passengers took photogaphs and enjoyed the panorama. Now there is a 15-minute time-limit on parking on the Piazzale, and only a certain number of buses are allowed to occupy the space at any one time.

Inside Museo della Foundazione Horne

At the next junction it's worth taking a small detour to the right, down Via de' Neri to the church of ★**San Remigio** 82 (open for services only), consecrated to St Remigius (Saint-Rémy) of Reims. After the simple facade, the French Gothic three-aisled interior comes as quite a surprise (13th to 14th-century): it has dichromatic pointed-arch arcades, and a ribbed vault. The most striking fresco here is the *Madonna Enthroned*, attributed to the Cimabue school (13th-century).

At the intersection on the way back to Via de' Benci lies the **Museo della Fondazione Horne** 83 (open Mon–Sat 9am–1pm), presented to Florence by the English art historian Herbert Horne (1864–1916). This collection of painting, sculpture and historic furniture contains a fine *St Stephen* attributed to Giotto, and also a book containing sketches by Tiepolo (18th-century).

From Via de' Benci, the **Ponte alle Grazie** leads across the Arno into the San Niccolò quarter. On the left side of the Piazza de' Mozzi stands the **Museo Bardini** 84 (closed for restoration), built in the 19th century, which contains large collections of sculpture, paintings and tapestries.

The pretty Via di San Niccolò leads past the church of **San Niccolò sopr'Arno** 85 – Michelangelo hid from the German occupiers in its campanile in 1530 – and then comes out at the **Porta San Niccolò** 86, a tower from the city's third wall, dating from 1324.

SAN MINIATO AL MONTE

Winding steps now lead up to the ★★**Piazzale Michelangelo**, a viewing platform opened in 1875. A bronze copy of Michelangelo's *David* is surrounded here by copies of the *Four Seasons* from the Medici Chapels.

Past the restaurant loggia at the back, steps lead to the church of San Salvatore al Monte by Cronaca (1475), and then up to ★★**San Miniato al Monte** 87, one of the oldest churches in the city (open daily, summer: 8am–noon, 2–7pm; winter: 8am–noon, 2.30–6pm). It was started in 1018, and is a fine example of Florentine Romanesque, reminiscent of the Baptistry. The facade is highly decorative: its five arches bear no relation to the three-aisled basilica inside; the sloping diagonals at the sides of the triangular gable iron out the architectural contradiction.

Star Attractions
- **Piazzale Michelangelo**
- **San Miniato al Monte**

INTERIOR

The open timber roof is lent rhythm by alternating groups of columns, drawing the eye towards the mosaic of Christ in the apse. Just before the magnificent rood screen is the elegant ★ **Cappella del Crocifisso**, a tiny vaulted temple with pillars, terracotta and paintings. Michelozzo worked here with Luca della Robbia, and the paintings are by Agnolo Gaddi (1394–6). Another successful Florentine joint venture was the Cappella del Cardinale di Portogallo (left aisle). Brunelleschi's pupil Manetti built this funeral chapel (1461–6) for the Cardinal of Lisbon, who died in Florence. The ceiling has five medallions by Luca della Robbia, and the frescoes are by Alesso Baldovinetti.

The Gothic sacristy contains a *Life of St Benedict* fresco by Spinello Aretino (late 14th-century). The 11th-century ★ **Crypt**, which houses the relics of St Minias, is the most important part of the building. The narrow Byzantine windows in the nave and the dichromatic marble are both characteristic features of Florentine Romanesque.

Below: apse mosaic of Christ in San Miniato
Bottom: city sunset

Badia Fiesolana marble

Excursion 1: Fiesole

Take bus No 7 via Stazione-Duomo-San Marco 7km/4 miles); car drivers should leave the city centre at the Piazza della L ibertà and travel along Via Don Giovanni Minzoni. Just outside the city is **San Domenico** with its church and convent (founded 1406), where Fra Beato Angelico, the painter-monk, used to live; when the convent took over San Marco down in the city he was given an important task *(see page 81)*. The convent church contains a *Madonna with Angels and Saints* by Fra Angelico (c 1430) in the first side-chapel on the left (the architectural background was added by Lorenzo di Credi in 1501) and the convent's chapter house contains a *Crucifixion* fresco by Fra Angelico (c 1440).

BENEDICTINE BADIA

At the traffic lights, the road goes left in the direction of **Badia Fiesolana** (Fiesole Abbey; open Mon–Fri 9am–5pm, Sat 9am–noon). For four centuries, from 1028 until 1437, it was a Bene-

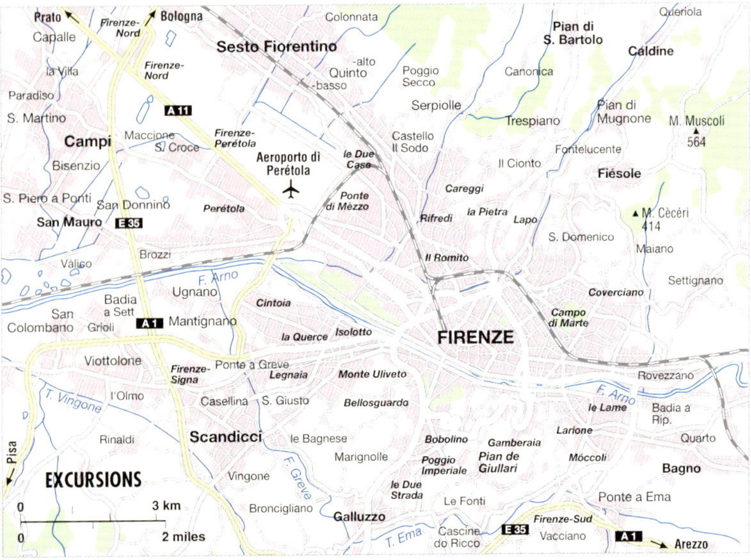

dictine house. The unfinished facade dates from the 11th century, and its dichromatic marble is reminiscent of the Baptistry and San Miniato. Otherwise, the church and convent are Renaissance: Cosimo the Elder had them altered, Brunelleschi-style, after 1437, and turned the Badia into a meeting-place for artists and scholars. The buildings today house the European University Institute, and those who live and work here have breathtaking views of Florence.

Ancient Fiesole
Archaeologists have found Etruscan remains in Fiesole dating from the 7th century BC. Under the Roman Empire the town was given a capitol, a theatre and thermal baths. It flourished as an independent city through the Dark Ages, and it was not until 1125 that Florence finally succeeded in annexing its neighbour.

THE CATHEDRAL

The road then winds away from San Domenico and uphill to the Piazza of **Fiesole** (Roman *Faesulae*), a former Etruscan city. The campanile dominating the piazza is reminiscent of the one on the Palazzo Vecchio; in fact it dates from 1213, and the one in Florence was modelled after it. Behind its rather unattractive facade, the cathedral of **San Romolo** (open daily 8am–noon, 4–6pm) contains a three-aisled, bare stone interior dating back to 1028; it was altered in the 13th century. The raised choir lies above the hall crypt, with its archaic capitals and columns. The Cappella Salutati (on the right-hand side of the presbytery) contains some fine work by Mino da Fiesole (c 1431–84), and the large altarpiece above the high altar is by Bicci di Lorenzo (1450).

Below: San Romolo facade
Bottom: San Francesco ceiling

SAN FRANCESCO

Opposite the facade is the Bishop's Palace, to the left of which a very steep, paved lane leads up to the site of the Etruscan and later Roman acropolis. On the way up there are some superb views of Florence. The lane goes past the 6th-century church of **Sant'Alessandro** (closed, only open when there are exhibitions running), built on the site of a Bacchic temple. The marble columns of this three-aisled building are Roman.

At the very top of the hill, on the site of the former acropolis, stand the convent buildings of **San Francesco** (open daily 9.30am–12.30pm, 3–6pm). The simple little church with its single

Map on page 98

aisle and vaulted ceiling contains some fine 15th-century paintings. A steep flight of steps leads down to the Missionary Museum, which has a collection of Etruscan and Roman (as well as Egyptian and Chinese) exhibits.

Fragments of Fiesole
Etrusco-Roman Fiesole has yielded a wealth of finds – statues, sculpture, ceramics, coins, architectural fragments – and most of them are on display in the Archaeological Museum beside the theatre (opening times as for the theatre). The building is an imaginative reconstruction of the 1st-century BC Roman temple, whose excavated remains can be seen in the northwest corner of the theatre complex.

ARCHAEOLOGICAL EXCAVATIONS

Behind the cathedral is the **Museo Bandini**, containing terracotta of the della Robbia school and panels of the Tuscan school (14th–15th-century); and in the same street (Via Dopre) is the **Museo Primo Conti**, dedicated to the eponymous 20th-century Florentine painter, and containing a collection of documents concerning many other avant-garde Italian artists (open Mon and Wed–Sat 10am–1pm).

Beyond is the **Teatro Romano** (Roman Theatre, open daily 9am–7pm, in winter: 9am–5pm). The structure here once held around 25,000 spectators, and it is one of the oldest Roman theatres (1st-century BC). The raised stage, 26m (85ft) wide, can be easily made out. Further down the hill the remains of some Roman baths have been excavated; there are chambers of varying sizes, including a room where the water was heated, dating from the time of Hadrian (117–138). To the left of the theatre is a temple area, with remains of a Roman temple and also a mighty Etruscan one (3rd-century BC). Across the whole area is a long Etruscan city-wall; its impressive, rough-hewn masonry contrasts with the more finely-structured Roman walls.

Teatro Romano

Excursion 2: Prato

Numerous trains travel to the town of Prato (20km/13 miles) from Florence's main station (buy a ticket to *Prato Centrale*). Buses run by the firm of Lazzi also do direct trips, and leave from outside the station. Car drivers should take the A1 in the direction of Bologna as far as the Prato-Calenzano exit, or the country road via Sesto Fiorentino (leave the ring road at the Piazza Costituzione). The area around Prato (which means meadow) has been inhabited since Palaeolithic times. During the Middle Ages, Prato was an independent city-state with its own flourishing textile and silk industries, until it was swallowed up by Florence in 1351.

The town remained wealthy, however, as evidenced by the magnificent works of art to be found here. Prato also has a famous son: Francesco di Marco Datini (died 1410) was an Italian international merchant and banker, whose business and private papers, preserved here in Prato, constitute one of the most important archives of the economic history of the Middle Ages.

★

Star Attraction

• outdoor pulpit

Below: the outdoor pulpit on the cathedral of Santo Stefano
Below: the cloisters

PRATO CATHEDRAL

All that remains of the original 12th-century ★ **Cathedral of Santo Stefano** (open Mon–Sat 7am–12.30pm, 3.30–7pm, Sun 7am–1pm, 3.30–8pm) are the campanile and the cloister; the facade in dichromatic marble was only built in 1385. The ★★ **outdoor pulpit** on the facade is an architectural rarity. It is where the *Sacra Cintola*, or Holy Girdle, is venerated five times annually (Easter, 1 May, 15 August, especially 8 September, and Christmas). Donatello did some fine marble reliefs for the balustrade (1434–8), and the pulpit itself is by Michelozzo (the original parapet is in the Cathedral Museum).

Map on page 98

Below: Santo Stefano's campanile
Bottom: the rooftops of Prato

BELL TOWER

The ★ **campanile** is also worth a closer look: because of the extension work during the 13th century it is now jammed between the nave and transept, and the original way through it via the ground floor had to be walled up. Above are three Romanesque double-mullioned windows *(bifore)* and above them, two far more eye-catching storeys. The top one is Gothic (1340–56) while the lower one, which used to be the belfry, has had its decoration adapted but its Romanesque arches retained. It is this unusual combination that gives the campanile of Prato Cathedral its unique appearance.

The interior, with its dichromatic accentuation of the arches, was certainly a novelty at the time it was built (1211). The cup-shaped ★ **marble pulpit** is by Mino da Fiesole and Antonio Rossellino (1473). Mino designed it and did two of the skilfully carved scenes (*Banquet of Herod* and *Martyrdom of St John the Baptist*), Rossellino did the other scenes and the workshop took care of the fine sculpture at the base of the pulpit.

FINE FRESCOES

The transept is a Gothic extension attributed to Giovanni Pisano (as are the extra storeys on the campanile), and was completed in 1317. The pres-

bytery contains one of the finest ★★ **fresco cycles** of the early Renaissance: Filippo Lippi painted the ★***Life of St John the Baptist*** here and designed the stained-glass windows between 1452 and 1466; the banquet scene, with the guests wearing costumes from Lippi's time, and the graceful Salome are justly famous. The cathedral also contains ★**frescoes** by Paolo Uccello and Agnolo Gaddi, as well as sculpture by Giovanni Pisano, Benedetto da Maiano, Ferdinando Tacca, and many others.

CATHEDRAL MUSEUM

To the left of the facade is the entrance to the Cathedral Museum, or ★**Museo dell'Opera del Duomo** (open Mon and Wed–Sat 9.30am–12.30pm, 3–6.30pm; Sun 9.30am–12.30pm), which contains Donatello's original dancing *putti* for the outdoor pulpit, as well as frescoes, liturgical objects and altar panels. The inner courtyard provides access to the former ★**cloister**, one side of which has been preserved in its entirety: with its polychrome marble and elegant, finely-structured capitals, it is a rare example of the Byzantine-Romanesque style in Tuscany (late 12th-century). There is access from here to the interesting ★**crypt**.

On the site of the mighty *fortezza*, that Frederick II of Germany had built here in 1248 (Prato was friendly to the emperor), stands a rather unprepossessing square structure, with a round roof and lantern above its unfinished exterior – **Santa Maria delle Carceri** (open daily 7am–noon, 4–7pm). The ★**interior**, however, is one of the main works of the Renaissance period and is by Giuliano da Sangallo (1484–92). This centralised, domed building in the shape of a Greek cross is reminiscent of Brunelleschi's Pazzi Chapel in Florence. A continuous balustrade runs around the wall; pilasters, circles and semicircles, and the classic contrast between light and dark stone, all contribute to the austerity of this interior, which is rounded off perfectly by colourful enamelled terracotta of the della Robbia school.

★

Star Attraction
• Cathedral frescoes

Cathedral frescoes
In Prato's Via Rinaldesca is the mid-14th-century frescoed Palazzo Datini (open Mon–Sat 9am–noon, also Tues and Thur 4–7pm), which offers a fascinating description of life in medieval Prato. It was the home of Francesco Datini, the founder of the city's riches in the wool trade, and the eponymous subject of Iris Origo's book *The Merchant of Prato.*

Cloister well

Art History

Archaeological finds have proved that the region occupied by present-day Florence was inhabited before the Roman colony was founded: impressive monuments testifying to the fact include the well-preserved Etruscan tombs, La Montagnola and La Mula, near Sesto Fiorentino. The exhibits in the city's Museo Archeologico document the finds from Roman *Florentia*. From the Middle Ages onwards, Florence developed its own very individual style of architecture.

THE PROTO-RENAISSANCE

Around the year 1060, construction work began on two sacred buildings: the Baptistry and San Miniato al Monte. Neither was based on the 'imperial' architectural style in the north known as Romanesque, but instead on very different traditions.

The centralised structure of the octagonal Baptistry is derived from Roman Antiquity, as are its dichromatic marble exterior (incrustation technique) and its formal language of semicircles and right-angles. This is also true of San Miniato al Monte, which is built on an Early Christian basilica marking the shrine of the Christian martyr St Minias. Its small, narrow windows are not Romanesque but Byzantine, an important architectural influence in Central Italy, preserving architectural elements of Antiquity; Florence did a great deal to cherish these traditions. This also applies to the church of SS Apostoli and the cathedral in Fiesole, which were both built at approximately the same time.

PAINTING

The orthodox link with Byzantine painting and its schematic representations was broken by the Florentine painters Cimabue (1240–1302) and Giotto (1266–1337), as well as by the Sienese painter Duccio di Buoninsegna (1255–1319). The stiffness and severity vanished for ever, and a

Tower houses

The most notable secular buildings in Florence during the early Middle Ages were the tall towers known as *case-torri*. The conflict between the Guelfs, supporters of the Pope, and the Ghibelline, allies of the Emperor, resulted in constant blood feuds from around 1215 onwards, and families built tall towers as safe refuges. There were over 150 of them at one time, many over 70 metres (230ft) high. After the constitutional reform of 1293, when the nobility lost their overriding influence, the towers were reduced to a maximum height of 30 metres (100ft) – which was still very high. Many examples of such towers survive in today's Florence.

Opposite: the Foundling Hospital courtyard
Below: San Miniato interior

fresh wind blew through the world of painting, with subjective depiction taking the place of objective representation. The themes remained the same, but there was a general shift from the symbolic to the personal.

Works by the three painters mentioned above can be admired in the Uffizi Palace, which also contains the greatest works of the Siena School, by the brothers Ambrogio and Pietro Lorenzetti (both died 1348) and by Simone Martini (1285–1344).

Below: Santa Croce
Bottom: frieze detail from the church of Orsanmichele

GOTHIC IN FLORENCE

The International Gothic style reached the city from north of the Alps, brought by the churches of the international mendicant orders: Santa Maria Novella (Dominican, 1246–78) and Santa Croce (Franciscan, 1295–1370). The Gothic style of both these churches tends to do its soaring sideways rather than heavenwards, and the rows of square chapels are typical of the orders. After the plague epidemic of 1348, the worried populace made donations which funded the building of Orsanmichele, that mixture of a church and a palace. The ground floor of the church is a triumph of spiritual Gothic, while the style of the upper floors is reminiscent of the double windows of the Palazzo Vecchio.

RENAISSANCE FLORENCE

At the beginning of the 15th century (the Italian *Quattrocento*), a new philosophy of life seemed to flood through the city: the spiritual interlude was being replaced by a new realism. In 1401 Lorenzo Ghiberti (1378–1455) won a competition, in which Filippo Brunelleschi (1377–1446) also took part, for the design of the second door of the Baptistry. The quartet of great sculptors was completed by Donatello (1386–1466) and Nanni di Banco (1380–1421).

Della Robbia

The Florentine sculptor Luca della Robbia (1399–1482) made a great contribution to the expressiveness of the medium. He founded a family studio primarily associated with the production of works in polychrome enamelled terracotta, the earliest of his works in this medium being the lunette of the *Resurrection* (1442–5), over the door of the northern sacristy of the Duomo. His most famous work is the charming *Cantoria* (choir loft) now in the Museo dell'Opera del Duomo.

BRUNELLESCHI AND DONATELLO

Of the four, it was Brunelleschi who was to have the greatest impact on the architecture of the city. Though he lost the competition for the design of the Baptistry door, he did win another competition: the one for the cathedral dome in 1418.

Brunelleschi had already closely examined the city's architectural styles, studied the literature of Antiquity and rediscovered the principles of linear-perspective construction known to the Greeks and Romans. His architecture, which can be seen to greatest effect in San Lorenzo, the Foundling Hospital, the Pazzi Chapel and in Santo Spirito, makes use of the formal principles of the classical art of Antiquity. The *pietra serena*, that grey sandstone he used for his buildings, combines with the white walls to create the formal harmony so characteristic of architecture in Florence. Brunelleschi also used an ancient Roman construction technique to build the cathedral dome, placing the brickwork in herringbone patterns between a framework of stone beams.

Below: model of Brunelleschi's dome

Donato de' Bardi, or Donatello, helped sculpture break the bonds of Gothic formalism and gave it a whole new lease of Renaissance life. Apart from two brief stays in Rome, to study Antiquity, and in Padua, Donatello lived his whole life (1386–1466) in Florence and left behind works that made him the greatest sculptor of his generation. Of his works in the Museo dell'Opera del Duomo, the prophets *Jeremiah* and *Habakuk* (the latter also known as *Zuccone*, or pumpkin, because of his bald head) display the psychological realism of his early period (until c 1430) and the individual way in which Renaissance artists rendered the human form.

Donatello's *Maddalena*, which he did when he was almost 70, dispenses with aesthetic beauty entirely and – in wood this time – concentrates instead on incredibly direct emotional appeal.

Below: detail of a Masaccio fresco in the Brancacci Chapel
Bottom: Palazzo Vecchio

PERSPECTIVE IN PAINTING

The painter Masaccio (1401–28) died young, but his frescoes had a huge effect on the Early Renaissance. He devoted himself – probably in the company of Brunelleschi and Donatello – to the study of perspective (see his *Fresco of the Trinity* in Santa Maria Novella) and used light and shade to create entirely new spatial effects in painting (Brancacci Chapel). This accounts for the relaxed and natural effect of Masaccio's group compositions, the perfect aesthetics of which so impressed Leonardo da Vinci, Michelangelo and Raphael.

Masaccio's contemporary Paolo Uccello (1399–1475) also used the new perspective to great effect (*Battaglia di San Romano*, Uffizi; *Equestrian memorial to Sir John Hawkwood* in the Duomo). Also part of the same generation were the great painters Domenico Veneziano (c 1400–61) and Fra Filippo Lippi (1406–69).

THE FLORENTINE PALAZZO

The Palazzo di Bargello (1255) and the Palazzo Vecchio (1299) marked the start of an architectural development that was later to influence all Europe. These massive, battlemented medieval fortress-buildings were originally constructed to house the *Capitano del Popolo* (Bargello) and the *priori* (Vecchio), and needed to be able to withstand attack. Built in *pietra forte* on trapezoidal ground-plans, these imposing structures, with their graceful divided windows and battlemented galleries, symbolised the power of the city's rulers.

The architects of the family palazzi in the 15th century used the same design, but in a somewhat modified form: the tower disappeared and the battlements gave way to artistically moulded ledges and cornices. A good example is the Palazzo Strozzi (1489), its central portal flanked by square windows, and the heavy rustication arranged more creatively than defensively. The divided windows on the first floor, with their characteristic 'eyebrows', are more artistically done than those on the second. In stark contrast to the gravity of the exterior is the delicacy of the inner courtyard, which is lined by arcades giving access to all the rooms.

Alberti

A special role in the Early Renaissance was played by the architectural theorist Leon Battista Alberti (1404–72). Like his friend Brunelleschi, Alberti, a doctor of law, studied the artistic theories of the ancients. His *Ten Books on Architecture*, based on his long study of Vitruvius, became a bible of Renaissance architecture. He designed the Palazzo Rucellai, with its rusticated masonry and its three superimposed architectural orders in the pilasters, as well as the facade of Santa Maria Novella.

THE SECOND GENERATION

The artistic achievements of the Florentine Early Renaissance in painting and sculpture took place during the first few decades of the 15th century. After the death of Donatello (1466), a second generation of artists began to show an inclination towards an art of affirmation, reflected in the opulent court of Lorenzo the Magnificent (1469–92). The bold line-up of contemporary figures in the Sassetti Chapel in Santa Trinità, by Domenico Ghirlandaio (1449–94), betrays an attitude very different from that of Masaccio's paintings in the Brancacci Chapel. The sculptor Andrea Verrocchio (1435–88), and the painters Fra Filippo Lippi (1457–1504) and Sandro Botticelli (1444–1510), were part of this generation.

Mythological figures taken from Antiquity appeared for the first time in painting (Botticelli's

Below: window in the Palazzo Rucellai
Bottom: Adoration of the Magi *by Ghirlandaio*

Birth of Venus in the Uffizi), and the Dominican monk Savonarola declared open war on secularisation – deeply impressing Botticelli, Michelangelo (1475–1564) and many others.

Below: Giambologna's Rape of the Sabine Women
Bottom: Botticelli's Birth of Venus

THE 16TH CENTURY

The early work by Michelangelo in the Casa Buonarroti already reveals the later master. Even though he worked for the Medici (New Sacristy of San Lorenzo 1520–34, Biblioteca Laurenziana 1524) he never lost sight of his basic principles, so well expressed by his *Schiavi* (Slaves) in the Accademia. His world-famous works include the *Tondo Doni* of the Holy Family (Uffizi), his *Pietà* in the Museo dell'Opera del Duomo, and his *David* (Accademia – copy in the Palazzo Vecchio), which was originally commissioned as the first of 12 statues of the prophets for the cathedral choir. Michelangelo helped fortify his city when Florence was besieged by Charles V's army, but all in vain. In 1530, four years after the Medici had established themselves, he left Florence for good.

Among those who remained were the goldsmith Benvenuto Cellini (1500–71), a copy of whose *Perseus* can be seen adorning the Loggia dei Lanzi, the sculptor Giambologna (1529–1608), who created the *Equestrian statue of Cosimo I* and also the *Rape of the Sabine Women*

(both in the Piazza della Signoria), and also the painters Jacopo Pontormo (1494–1556) and Rosso Fiorentino (1494–1540), both considered leading exponents of Mannerism.

LITERATURE

Like painting, literature in Florence also experienced a sudden change during the Early Renaissance, when the Tuscan dialect was elevated to a new literary level by Dante Alighieri (1265–1321). He also wrote in Latin, but his *Divina Commedia* (Divine Comedy), a journey through hell, purgatory and paradise in 100 cantos, established Tuscan as the literary vernacular of Italy. As a poet (sonnets and *canzoni*) Dante belonged to the *dolce stil novo* (the sweet new style), which articulated human sentiment in popular dialect. Dante's contemporary Giovanni Villani (1276–1348) wrote a chronicle of his native city that is an authentic historical source.

The next generation cultivated Humanism, and the literature of ancient Greek and Rome played a major role in Florentine intellectual life. Giovanno Boccaccio (1313–75) wrote his Decameron and also commentaries on Dante's Commedia; Petrarch (1304–74) wrote some superb lyric poetry. Both of them collected the work of Greek authors. The Medici played their part in promoting Humanism in literature. Cosimo the Elder (1389– 1464) came into contact with the Greek world at the Council of Florence (where Byzantium asked for help against the Ottomans, to no avail). In 1439 he founded a Platonic academy in Florence. His nephew Lorenzo the Magnificent (1449–92) surrounded himself with philosophers and poets, and also wrote some quite respectable poetry of his own.

During his exile, Niccolò Machiavelli (1469–1527), head of the second chancery (1498–1512), wrote his epoch-making political work *Il Principe* (The Prince). As a poet he also wrote the first Italian character comedy, *La Mandragola* (c 1520).

The Accademia della Crusca, founded in 1586, printed the first Italian dictionary in Florence in 1612.

The birth of opera

The nobles of Florence were patrons not only of art and literature, but of music too. In 1580, a society of poets and musicians known as the *Camerata Florentina* met in Florence, under the patronage of Count Giovanni Bardi, to revive Greek tragedy and recreate the lost harmony of language and music. Their efforts resulted in the development of monody – in contrast to the polyphonic music of that time – and led to the composition of what is aguably the first opera, *Daphne* (1597), by Iacopo Peri. The new style soon became popular, and in Mantua Claudio Monteverdi (1567–1643) wrote his *Orfeo*, the earliest opera to survive.

Dante

Music, Theatre and Festivals

Florence has a thriving cultural scene, with opera, concert and ballet events of a high international standard. The Teatro Comunale is the main venue for opera and ballet, staging performances according to the seasons: October to December – opera; January to April – concerts and ballet; May to June – *Maggio Musicale*; July – summer season.

The theatres in Florence usually feature performances by visiting troupes, though there is the odd Florentine production too – Machiavelli's comedies, for example.

To keep up-to-date with events, buy *Firenze Spettacolo* (available from newsstands), the monthly listings magazine. Although it is in Italian, the listings themselves are quite straightforward. Alternatively, obtain *Events* (free from the tourist office and available in English). *Concierge Information* is another useful bi-monthly publication available in hotels.

Concerts of popular and classical music are held regularly, often in churches or in the open air. The Orchestra Regionale della Toscana (ORT), tel: 055-281792, and the Filarmonica di Firenze 'Gioacchino Rossini' are the two principal orchestras based in Florence.

The *Maggio Musicale* festival, held from mid-May to the end of June, is a big event, with top

Below: authentic performance
Bottom: festival reveller

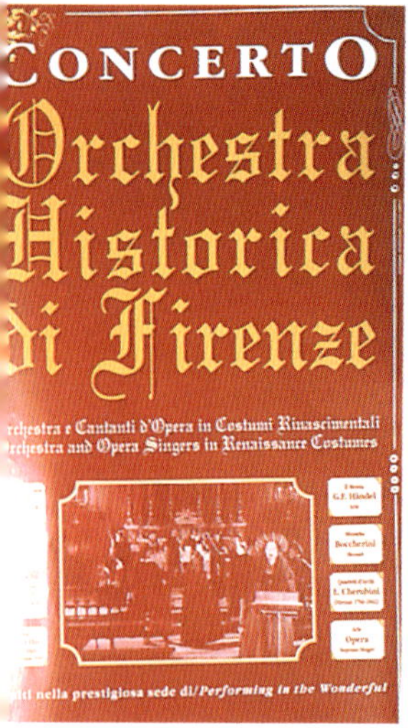

names in music, ballet and opera performing in various venues throughout the city, including the Piazza della Signoria. Tickets can be had from the Teatro Comunale, Corso Italia 16, box office 055-211158 or 213535, www.maggiofiorentino.com. Concerts are held throughout the summer in cloisters, piazzas or the Boboli Gardens.

During the *Estate Fiesolana* – Fiesole's summer festival (June to August) – concerts, opera, ballet and theatre are held in the Roman theatre and other venues.

Classical concerts are also held in many churches. To find out what rock, jazz and Latin American music is on offer, check in the latest issue of *Firenze Spettacolo*.

On stage
The main theatres are the Teatro della Pergola, Via della Pergola 18, tel: 055-2264316 and Teatro Verdi, Via Ghibellina 99, tel: 055-2638777 or 055-212320. Most productions are in Italian.

POPULAR FESTIVALS

Scoppio del Carro (on Easter Sunday): literally, the 'exploding cart'. A wheeled pagoda several metres high pulled by two garlanded white oxen, covered with fireworks and topped with a crown, stops before the Duomo. From the high altar a 'dove', aided by a wire, swoops through the open door and strikes the cart, at which point the fireworks explode. The festival dates back to medieval times.

Festa del Grillo (Cricket Festival, held on the weekend after Ascension). The city park, *Le Cascine*, is a hive of activity, with people chasing crickets or buying them ready-caught in tiny cages. The insect has been regarded since antiquity as a fertility symbol and a good-luck charm, but now animal activists are trying to ban the use of live crickets in the festival.

Calcio storico (historic football tournament) with the final being held on the 24 June (a public holiday), followed by fireworks at the Piazzale Michelangelo. This is also the name-day of the city's patron saint, John the Baptist. The competition is held to commemorate the game played in 1530, when the German occupying team lost to the Florentines, and the tradition is kept up annually in historic costume on the Piazza Santa Croce *(see page 95)*.

Medieval revival

FOOD AND DRINK

Tuscany offers some of the finest food in Italy. When Catherine de' Medici married Henry II of France in 1533 and moved her court to Paris, she took her Tuscan chefs and recipes with her, thus laying the foundation for French *haute cuisine*.

Of course, like any other city, Florence will also provide you with a bland three-course *menù turistico* at an all-in price (usually around €20), and it has its share of self-service restaurants too, with names like *Tavola Calda, Self-Service, Buffet, Rosticceria*, etc.

Pizza in Florence is even sold by the slice on the street *(al taglio)* and is usually accompanied by beer. One name to look out for is *friggitoria*: these are small shops where delicious fried snacks are sold.

TUSCAN COOKING

Numerous restaurants (usually *trattorie* or *osterie*) serve excellent food in an unfussy way. Genuine Tuscan cuisine is a wonderful mixture of simplicity and refinement: after a powerful bread soup *(ribollita)*, baked pancakes *(crespelle)* arrive, melting in the mouth bewitchingly with their finely-spiced fillings.

Or you might start with *crostini*, toasted slices of white bread topped with liver pâté or spicy tomato purée, followed by a choice of pasta. If you don't want to fill up on pasta, you can ask for a half-portion *(mezza porzione)* or a little to try *(assaggini)* – the Italians do this all the time. Pasta sauces are often based on vegetables, e.g. *asparagi* (asparagus), *melanzane* (aubergine) and *zucchini*.

Arista is a finely-spiced piece of roast pork. In autumn, game and mushrooms from the surrounding hills adorn the tables, and seafood is available all year round. Tripe is particularly popular; street vendors provide various different types of sandwich *(panini)* often containing delicious *trippa alla Fiorentina*. *Lampredotto* is a very popular dish – tripe in a roll with *salsa verde*.

Bar meals

There are many alternatives to a full restaurant meal, especially at lunchtime. Many local bars serve pasta, some meat dishes and salads, and wine bars (*enoteche* or *vinaie*) often supply snacks or more substantial dishes; usually inexpensive, they're invariably better than in a touristy *Tavola Calda*.

WINES

Florence is surrounded by vineyards and the whole of Tuscany is one enormous wine-growing region, producing many types of wine, but Chianti in particular. Made from several different grapes, Chianti varies in taste considerably, its bouquet ranging from dry violet to fully-rounded velvet.

Chianti classico is the wine whose origin is the hills to the south of Florence; *Chianti putto* comes from the Pistoia region; and *Chianti Rufina* is made in the wine areas to the east, on the slopes of the Apennines.

Other top red Tuscan wines include *Brunello di Montalcino* and *Nobile di Montepulciano*. A delicious white is the *Vernaccia di San Gimignano*, from the famous town between Florence and Siena.

Wine lovers should look out for the *Cantine Aperte* day – usually the last Sunday in May – when numerous wineries throw open their doors to the public for tours and tastings.

Restaurant selection

We have divided restaurants into three categories, based on prices:

€€€ = expensive
€€ = moderate
€ = inexpensive

Beccofino, Piazza degli Scarlatti (Lungarno Guicciardini), tel: 055-290076. Wine bar and restaurant in one big space, serving a good choice of creative fish and meat dishes. Contemporary décor (a refreshing change from the norm). Closed Monday. **€€€.**
Caffè Concerto, Lungarno C. Colombo 7, tel: 055-677377. With picture windows that look onto the river and a warmly-lit, plant-filled interior, this restaurant makes a romantic spot from which to sample creative Italian cooking. Closed Sunday. **€€€.**
Cavolo Nero, Via del Ardiglione 22, tel: 055-294744. Laid-back atmosphere and good Tuscan food (with the odd twist) in the Oltrarno. **€€€.**
Cibreo, Via dei Macci 118r, tel: 055-2341100. This classy restaurant, one of the best-known in Florence, serves classic Tuscan dishes in an elegant yet unstuffy atmosphere. Trattoria Cibreo next door serves the same dishes at a third of the price in a much more casual setting. Closed Sunday and Monday. **€€€.**
Don Chisciotte, Via C. Ridolfi 4r, tel: 055-475430. Creative Italian food with an emphasis on fish. **€€€.**
Enoteca Pinchiorri, Via Ghibellina 87, tel: 055-24277. In a class of its own, this 2 Michelin-starred restaurant is one of the best in the country. Located in a Renaissance *palazzo* with a beautiful courtyard for summer eating, it serves both Tuscan and international dishes, and has an exceptional wine list. Expect to pay L150,000 plus wine. Closed Tuesday lunchtime and Sunday and Monday. **€€€.**
Oliviero, Via delle Terme 51r, tel: 055-212421. Creative without being too fussy, Tuscan and Italian dishes are served in an ambiance that is a throwback to the fifties. Closed Sunday. **€€€.**
Pane e Vino, Via San Niccolò 70r, tel: 055-2476956. A pleasant, relaxed restaurant serving creative Tuscan dishes and offering an excellent wine list. The set menu is great value. Closed Sunday. **€€€.**
Da Stefano, Località Galluzzo, Via Senese 271, tel: 055-2049105. Out of town on the way to the motorway to Siena, this is a must for fish. Closed Sunday and lunchtimes. **€€€.**

A choice of pasta

Zibibbo, Via di Terzollina 3r, tel: 055-433383. Some way from the centre of town; Florentine classics are served in a colourful setting overlooking the city. Closed Sunday and Monday. **€€€**.
Baldini, Via Il Prato 96r, tel: 055-287663. A genuine family run trattoria. Closed Saturday and Sunday evenings. **€€**.
Baldovino, Via S. Giuseppe 22r, tel: 055-241773. A lively, often crowded restaurant with colourful décor, which serves pizzas and salads as well as full meals. Closed Monday. **€€**.
Bibé, Via delle Bagnese 1r, tel: 055-2049085. Home-made Florentine classics are served in this friendly, farmhouse restaurant (and outside in the garden), just off the Siena road near Galuzzo. Closed Wednesday. **€€**.
Cammillo, Borgo San Jacopo 57r, tel: 055-212427. A bustling, classic trattoria with simple but robust regional dishes. Closed Wednesday and Thursday, part of December and January, and two weeks in August. **€€**.
Osteria di Santo Spirito, Piazza Santo Spirito 16r, tel: 055-2382383. This osteria serves hot and cold dishes with outside tables on one of the city's most beautiful squares. Open daily. **€€**.
Sostanza, Via del Porcellana 25r, tel: 055-212691. Long-established trattoria (founded 1869), very plain and down-to-earth but patronised by famous clients such as Ezra Pound and Ronald Reagan (in his acting days). Equally famous is the speciality *petto di pollo al burro*, chicken breast in butter. Closed Saturday and Sunday. **€€**.
Trattoria del Carmine, Piazza del Carmine 18r, tel: 055-218601. There is a huge choice of dishes on the menu at this traditional trattoria, which offers good food at very honest prices. Closed Sunday. **€€**.
Boccadama, Piazza Santa Croce 25–26r, tel: 055-243640. In a lovely setting looking onto Piazza Santa Croce, this informal wine bar serves a good selection of cold dishes as well as more substantial fare. Closed Monday. **€**.
La Casalinga, Via Dei Michelozzi 9r, tel: 055-218624. A solid, fairly-priced trattoria with plentiful helpings of good home cooking and fast, friendly service. Closed Sunday. **€**.
Da Sergio, Piazza San Lorenzo 8r, tel: 055-281941. Simple Florentine dishes are served at communal tables in this trattoria, which is popular with the stall-holders of San Lorenzo market. Open for lunch only. Closed Sunday. **€**.
Fuoriporta, Via Monte Alle Croci 10r, tel: 055-2342483. One of the best wine bars in the centre, with an excellent selection of local dishes. Closed Sunday. **€**.
Il Pizzaiuolo, Via de' Macci 113r, tel: 055-241171. Offering one of the best pizzas in town, this place is always full and noisy. Good pastas and fish dishes too. Closed Sunday. **€**.
Tarocchi, Via dei Renai 14r, tel: 055-234391. Lively and friendly pizzeria popular with young Florentines. Closed Monday. **€**.
Trattoria Za-Za, Piazza Mercato Centrale 26r, tel: 055-215411. Hearty food served in a riotous atmosphere, with such staples as *ribollita, arista* and bean delicacies. Closed Sunday and all of August. **€**.

Ice cream
No visit to Florence would be complete without tasting an ice cream made on the premises. Always choose ice cream parlours *(gelaterie)* with a *Produzione Propria* (home-made) sign or credentials. Good *gelaterie* are **Perché No**, Via Tavolini 19r, near the Cathedral, **Gelateria Carabé**, Via Ricasoli 60r, and **Gelateria Ricchi**, Piazza Santo Spirito. **Vivoli**, Via Isola delle Stinche 7r, is the most famous of them all. Try the selection of *semifreddi* (ice cream and sponge desserts).

SHOPPING

Markets in Florence are great fun. The best include **San Lorenzo** (weekdays and Saturdays), which offers a fine selection of textiles, leather and souvenirs; the **Mercato delle Pulci** (Flea Market) on the Piazza dei Ciompi for junk; the market of **Sant'Ambrogio** (Piazza Ghiberti) for textiles, shoes, flowers and food (Monday to Saturday); and the huge **Cascine** (Tuesday mornings) for everything from live chickens to designer seconds and handbags, on Via delle Cascine, along the river to the west of the city.

CRAFTS

To see craftsmen at work, ask the Tourist Office for specific workshops or simply explore the Oltrarno quarter around Via Maggio. Leather-workers can be seen at the **Santa Croce leather school**, Piazza Santa Croce.

LEATHER

For top quality start with the designer boutiques in Via de' Tornabuoni or around the Piazza della Repubblica. For cheaper goods, there's the market of San Lorenzo. Or try **Raspini**, Via Roma 25–29, for superb leather bags and coats as well as high quality fashions; **Il Bisonte**, Via del Paione 31r, for chunky bags, luggage and other leather goods at high prices; **Furla**, Via Tosinghi 5r, for bags and accessories in contemporary designs.

Fashion boutiques
Florence is a high-spot for fashion, and the city centre is full of top designer boutiques. The most elegant streets are **Via de' Tornabuoni** and **Via della Vigna Nuova**, where Versace, Valentino, Armani, YSL, Coveri and all the other big fashion names have their outlets. Other exclusive streets are the **Via Calzaiuoli** and **Via Roma** (both have a stunning range of leather goods) and **Via del Parione**.

JEWELLERY

There is still a flourishing trade in gold (witness the Ponte Vecchio), but most pieces are now made in Arezzo. Try **Brandimarte**, Via Bartolini 18r, for handcrafted silver goods and jewellery at good prices, or **Gatto Bianco**, Borgo SS Apostoli 12r, for contemporary designs in gold and silver.

MARBLED PAPER

This is closely associated with Florence. Designs echo ancient themes or Medici crests. Visit **Giulio Giannini e Figlio**, Piazza Pitti 37r, Florence's longest-established paper shop, or **Il Papiro**, Via Cavour 55. At **Il Torchio**, Via de' Bardi 17, you can buy and also see the artisans at work.

FABRICS

Antico Setificio, Via L. Bartolini 4. This wonderful craft shop specialises in fabrics produced along traditional lines, especially silk. Try **Casa dei Tessuti**, Via de' Pecori, 20–24, for charming silks, linens and woollens.

SHOES

Ferragamo, Via de' Tornabuoni 16. Italy's most prestigious shoemaker provides hand-tooled shoes of all descriptions, and beautifully crafted ready-to-wear collections.
Cresti, Via Roma 9r, has beautifully made shoes for sale at much lower prices than Ferragamo.
Francesco, Via di Santo Spirito 62r, is the place for unpretentious shoes in classic designs handmade by a traditional craftsman.

PRACTICAL INFORMATION

Getting There

BY PLANE

One of the main airports for Florence is Pisa's Galileo Galilei International Airport. It is served by several charter companies (e.g. Italy Sky Shuttle), in addition to scheduled airlines such as Alitalia, Air France, Lufthansa, British Airways and Ryanair. The airport has a suburban railway connection with the main station of Santa Maria Novella (SMN) in Florence. Trains don't leave as frequently as you might expect and the journey takes about 55 minutes.

Many airlines now fly direct to Florence Peretola airport (also known as Amerigo Vespucci airport) only 6 km (4 miles) northwest of the city centre. Although these flights tend to be more expensive, many more now arrive here than in Pisa. The only UK flight is by Meridiana from London Gatwick. Cheaper flights to Bologna are also worth considering.

As yet, there are no direct flights between North America and Florence or Pisa. However, North America is well-connected to Florence via other major European cities. American and Canadian airlines operate to Fiumicino airport outside Rome, from where there are good rail connections to Florence.

BY RAIL

The main railway station in Florence, Santa Maria Novella, is served by fast intercity and sleeper connections from all over Europe. The train journey from London to Florence via Paris takes between 16 and 19 hours. If you enjoy rail travel, it's a pleasant journey, but no cheaper than flying.

BY CAR

Traffic arriving from the north reaches Florence via the Autostrada del Sole (A1) from Bologna, and there is also a motorway connection to Florence from the coastal cities of Livorno and La Spezia.

Anyone with time on their hands should avoid the very busy *tratto appenninico*, the section along the Apennines between Bologna and Florence, and instead take the SS 325, a pretty country road that runs to the

Florence is a high spot for fashion

west of the motorway. It ends up in Prato, right outside Florence.

Driving licences and vehicle registration documents are compulsory, as are warning triangles and the green insurance card in case of accidents. It's worth taking out a comprehensive insurance policy for the whole journey.

The maximum speed allowed on Italy's toll motorways is 130kph (80mph) for cars with capacities of over 1.1 litres; smaller vehicles may not travel faster than 110kph (68mph); and the usual limit on country roads is 90kph (56mph). Seat belts are compulsory in Italy.

Getting Around

BY CAR

In Florence it is best to park in one of the city's car parks. The boulevard ring around the city has signs all over it pointing the way to them. Since there aren't even enough spaces in the city centre for the local residents, it's best not even to try it, but instead to drive straight to the Parterre, the car park near Piazza Libertà. There is also a car park under Santa Maria Novella main station. Buses run from the Parterre into the city centre.

The *comune* of Florence now provides bicycles for use in the city centre. These cost virtually nothing and can be used from 8am–8pm. There are pick up points all over the city; Piazza Signoria. Bikes are a good way of exploring the historic centre, which is closed to cars and can only be driven through with a permit (though access to hotels is allowed). The police are notorious for towing cars away. Anyone who leaves their car in the street outside the centre should look out for signs saying *pulizia notturna*, which mean that the street is due to be cleaned that night, and vehicles are thus not allowed to park there after dark. Clamping has recently been introduced for unlawfully-parked cars.

As elsewhere in Italy, it's best not to tempt thieves by leaving any luggage or valuables in the car. Always lock all doors and close windows.

Taxis

These can be found all over the city They usually come quickly when called by phone (try 055-4798, 055-4390 or 055-4242); callers are given passwords. You will find taxi ranks in Via Pellicceria, Piazza de San Marco, Piazza Santa Maria Novella and Piazza Santa Trinità.

BY BUS

The bus network for Florence and environs is very comprehensive, and most lines pass the main station at some point. Tickets can be bought at *tabacchi*, newsstands or the automatic machines at the stops, which have instructions in four languages. Tickets must be validated in the orange machines at the back of the bus. Fewer buses run in the evenings, but there is a night service. There is also a fleet of electrically-powered mini-buses (A, B, C and D) which run routes around the *Centro Storico*; very useful for sight-seeing when your feet are tired.

HIRE CARS

All the big international car rental companies have branches in Florence, and can offer special weekend deals, unlimited mileage, etc. Information is available either from hotels or directly from the firms. It is worth remembering that it's often cheaper to book car hire before you arrive.

CITY SIGHTSEEING TOURS

These are organised by travel agencies. Several different programmes are available, some longer than others.

Facts for the Visitor

TRAVEL DOCUMENTS

Visitors from the US, EU and Commonwealth countries need only a passport for a stay of up to three months. Citizens of other countries should check with their nearest Italian consultate about obtaining a visa in advance of travel.

Police registration is required within three days of entering Italy; if you are staying in a hotel the management will do this on your behalf.

CUSTOMS

You're allowed to bring in as much currency as you like. Travelling from non-EU countries, you can bring 400 cigarettes, one bottle of spirits, two of wine and 50g of perfume; travelling from EU countries, there is no limit, provided goods are for your personal use. However, there are certain suggested limits to avoid problems: 800 cigarettes, 10 litres of spirits and 90 litres of wine.

Emergency numbers
Police immediate action: 112
Fire: 115
Ambulance: 118
General emergency: 113 (English-speaking operators in Florence and other major cities)
Automobile Club d'Italia (ACI)
24-hour breakdown: 116
24-hour information in English: 06 4477
Florence headquarters: 055-24861
Nighttime and holiday ambulance (*Misericordia)*, Piaza Duomo 2: 055-212222
Tourist Medical Service, 24-hour home visits by English- or French-speaking doctors: Via Lorenzo il Magnifico 59, tel: 055-475411
Car pound (if your car is towed away): 055-308249
Police Headquarters (in case of theft, lost passport etc): Via Zara 2, tel: 055-49771

FOREIGN EXCHANGE

Unlimited amounts of foreign currency and euros may be brought in and out of Italy, but need to be declared if the sum exceeds €10,500.

TIME

Italy is six hours ahead of US Eastern Standard Time and one hour ahead of Greenwich Mean Time. From March to October, like North America and the rest of Europe, Italy puts the clocks forward one hour.

INFORMATION

Information can be obtained from the offices of the Italian State Tourist Office (ENIT) at the following addresses:

In the UK: Italian State Tourist Office, 1 Princes Street, London W1, tel: 020 7408 1254; fax: 020 7493 6695; for brochures, tel: 0891 600280; website: www.enit.it/uk

In the US: Italian Government Tourist Office, 630 Fifth Avenue, Suite 1565, NY 10111, New York, tel: 212 245 4822; fax: 212 586 9249; website: www.italiantourism.com

In Florence: Via Cavour 1r, tel: 055-290832 (open Mon–Sat 8.15am–7.15pm; Mar–Oct: also Sun 8.15am–1.45pm); Piazza Stazione, tel: 055-212245 (open Mon–Sat 8.30am–7pm, Sun 8.30am–1.30pm); Borgo Santa Croce 29r, tel: 055-2340444 (open Mon–Sat 9am–2pm; Easter to end of Oct: Mon–Sat 9am–7pm, Sun 9am–1pm).

In Fiesole: Piazza Mino 37, tel: 055-5978373 (open Mon–Sat 8.30am–7.30pm, Sun 10am–7pm).

In Prato: Piazza Delle Carceri 15, tel: 0574-24112 (open Mon–Sat 9am–6.30pm).

CURRENCY

In February 2002, the euro (EUR) became the official currency used in

Italy, along with most other member states of the European Union. Euro notes are denominated in 5, 10, 20, 50, 100 and 500 euros; coins in 1 and 2 euros and 1, 2, 5, 10, 20 and 50 cents.

Banks and Exchange

Dollar or sterling travellers' cheques (preferably issued by a major bank or company such as Thomas Cook or American Express) can be used to obtain cash in any commercial bank, and in exchange for goods and services in shops and hotels. Expect to pay a small commission charge.

Most major credit/debit cards are accepted in hotels, restaurants and shops, for air and train tickets, and for cash in banks. For the best rates, change money and travellers' cheques at a bank (open 8.20am–1.20pm and 2.45–3.45pm). Better yet, avoid the queues and opening hours by drawing from the automated 'Bancomat' cash dispensers found at most banks.

If you are really hard up, go to American Express, Via Dante Alighieri 22r. The last resort should be any of the Ufficio Cambio, almost always offering the worst rates, despite the signs claiming 'no commission'.

Bills

Restaurants and other establishments are required by law (for tax reasons) to issue an official receipt to customers, who should not leave the premises without it.

Opening Times

Shops are open on weekdays from 9am–7.30pm, with a lunch break from 1–3.30pm. An increasing number of shops in the centre of town don't close at lunchtime. Also, many shops (again in the centre) are open for a few hours on Sundays, usually from 11am. Many shops are closed on Saturday and Monday afternoons.

Tipping

This is usually expected in restaurants even where service is included *(servizio compreso)*. A few euros are enough to show appreciation, though you should not tip unless you were happy with your meal. Hotel staff, taxi drivers, hairdressers and tour guides all expect to be tipped.

Museum opening hours vary considerably, and the times stated in this book are subject to change. Sights and museums are also liable to be closed for restoration. As far as possible, we have given warnings where this may be the case. Up-to-date information can be obtained from the tourist office.

Public Holidays

1 January (New Year); 6 January (Epiphany); Easter Monday; 25 April (Liberation Day); 1 May (Labour Day); 24 June (John the Baptist, Florence's patron saint); 15 August (Assumption of the Virgin or *Ferragosto*); 1 November (All Saints' Day); 8 December (the Immaculate Conception); 25–26 December (Christmas).

Post

The Central Post Office *(Palazzo delle Poste)* is at Via Pelliceria 160, under the arcades near the Piazza della Repubblica (open Mon–Fri 8.15am–7pm, Sat until noon), and there are several sub-branches (opening hours vary). You can also buy stamps *(francobolli)* at tobacconists *(tabacchi)*.

Telephoning

This can be done from public telephones, either with *gettoni* (phone tokens), coins or with phone cards (*carta telefonica*; break the tab off the card before first use), which can be purchased at tobacconists, most bars, newsstands and the post offices for €2.50, €5 or €7.50. It's a good idea to have both card and coins to hand. Bars and shops with a phone symbol sticking out from the wall above the door also have public phones.

To get an international line, dial 00. International dialling codes: Australia 61; France 33; Germany 49; Japan 81; Netherlands 31; Spain 34; United Kingdom 44; US and Canada 1.

When calling a Florence number, even from within the city itself, you must dial the full area code 055 as part of the number; and if you are calling from abroad, include the '0'.

VOLTAGE

220v; if you need an adaptor, buy it from a *ferramenta* shop.

HOUSE NUMBERS

Finding addresses can be confusing if the extra 'r' is overlooked; it stands for *rosso*, i.e. 'red', meaning that the address is a commercial enterprise. These have their own numbering system separate from the black numbers that are used for ordinary residential addresses.

SPORT

Florence has no shortage of sports facilities: there are swimming pools and facilities for tennis, rowing, horse-riding, plus an 18-hole golf course (addresses and opening hours can be found in the FCI pamphlet).

MEDICAL

Visitors from EU countries have the right to claim the health services available to Italians. UK visitors should obtain Form E111 from the Department of Health prior to departure.

Addresses of chemists open at night *(farmacie aperte 24 ore su 24)*, including the one at Florence station, are listed in the daily papers as well as in the windows of all other *farmacie*. A *farmacia* is identified by a sign displaying a red cross within a white circle. Normal opening hours are Monday to Friday 9am–1pm and 4pm–7pm.

Call the Tourist Medical Service, tel: 055-475411, for advice. The service is available 24 hours and a doctor will visit you in your hotel if necessary. In an emergency, dial 113 or 118 for an ambulance.

Every public hospital in Florence has a casualty department. The most central is the Ospedale Santa Maria Nuova in Piazza Santa Maria Nuova, tel: 055-27581.

THEFT

Keep a careful eye on your property at all times – theft is the order of the day. Documents and valuables should be kept in hotel safes, and it's advisable to take your radio with you when leaving your car.

The main emergency numbers (police, medical assistance) all over Italy are 112 and 113. The police headquarters in Florence are at Via Zara 2, tel: 055-49771.

DIPLOMATIC REPRESENTATION

British Consulate: Palazzo Castelbarco, Lungarno Corsini 2, Florence, tel: 055-212594.

American Consulate: Lungarno Amerigo Vespucci 38, Florence, tel: 055-2398276.

Free museums

The *Settimana del Beni Culturali*, or 'Free Museum Week', usually takes place in late February or early March. The state museums (including the Uffizi, Palatine, Accademia, Bergelio and many more) open to the public free of charge. Further information is available from tourist offices.

ACCOMMODATION

HOTELS AND GUEST HOUSES

Hotels *(alberghi)* are officially classed into five categories: luxury hotels, category I; category II; category III; and category IV. A list of hotels and boarding-houses showing the different prices can be obtained from tourist offices. Prices – even within the same category – vary considerably depending on location. To book a hotel, call the Florence Promotel agency (tel: 055-570481) or visit the ITA office at the main station. Note that it is advisable to book well in advance.

We have categorised accommodation into three groups:

€€€ = expensive
€€ = moderate
€ = inexpensive

Bernini Palace, Piazza San Firenze 29, tel: 055-288621. A small, refined hotel in a former mansion behind the Palazzo Vecchio. Breakfast is served in the Parliament Room, which housed the government when Florence was the capital of Italy. Private parking. **€€€**.

Brunelleschi, Piazza Santa Elisabetta 3, tel: 055-290322. Comfortable four-star hotel located in a tiny central square, and partly housed in a church with a 6th-century tower. **€€€**.

Excelsior, Piazza Ognissanti 3, tel: 055-264201. Old-world grandeur combined with modern conveniences in this former home of Napoleon's sister, Caroline. Polished service, luxurious rooms and fine views of the Arno from the roof-garden. Private parking. **€€€**.

Gallery Art Hotel, Vicolo dell'Oro 5, tel: 055-27263. A 65-room hotel within a stone's throw of the Ponte Vecchio, extensively redesigned in stunning style by Salvatori Ferragamo. Stylish modern restaurant serves French and Japanese cuisine. **€€€**.

Grand Hotel, Piazza Ognissanti 1, tel: 055-288781. Recently refurbished sister hotel to the Excelsior, and just as luxurious in terms of *fin-de-siècle* grandeur (with prices to match). **€€€**.

Grand Hotel Baglioni, Piazza Unità Italiana 6, tel: 055-23580. This classic hotel retains its air of discreet elegance, while providing extremely comfortable rooms. The rooftop restaurant has stunning views of the city skyline. **€€€**.

Florence has plenty of peaceful locations

Grand Hotel Villa Medici, Via Il Prato 42, tel: 055-2381331. An 18th-century palazzo with its own wooded gardens and pool. Most rooms have a terrace or balcony, and all have views of the gardens or the old city. **€€€.**
Helvetia & Bristol, Via dei Pescioni 2, tel: 055-287814. Small but grand hotel full of antiques and paintings, with sumptuous rooms, a winter garden, and gourmet restaurant. **€€€.**
Hermitage, Vicolo Marzio 1, Piazza del Pesce, tel: 055-287216. This intimate and engaging hotel close to the Ponte Vecchio has been furnished with antiques and oriental rugs by its English owners. Breakfast is served on the roof-terrace in summer. **€€€.**
Lungarno, Borgo San Jacopo 14, tel: 055-264211. Smart, comfortable modern hotel, very popular for its superb position on the river and views of the Ponte Vecchio from the front rooms. Restaurant specialises in fish. Private parking. **€€€.**
Minerva, Piazza Santa Maria Novella 16, tel: 055-27230. Four-star hotel situated right in front of Santa Maria Novella, overlooking the cloisters. Swimming pool on the panoramic terrace. Private parking. **€€€.**
Monna Lisa, Borgo Pinti 27, tel: 055-2479751. Small hotel (only 30 rooms) housed in a Renaissance palazzo which retains its original marble staircase, terracotta floors and painted ceilings. Many rooms overlook the lovely garden. **€€€.**
Regency, Piazza Massimo d'Azeglio 3, tel: 055-245247. Grand hotel in a 19th-century palazzo, with a highly-regarded restaurant and elegant garden. Private parking. **€€€.**
Savoy, Piazza Repubblica 7, tel: 055-283313. An elegant five-star hotel close to the main shopping area, refurbished to a high standard in 1986. **€€€.**
Torre di Bellosguardo, Via Roti Michelozzi 2, tel: 055-2298145. Set in the hills above Porta Romana, this quiet, roomy hotel consists of a 14th-century tower attached to a 16th-century villa. Frescoed reception rooms, antiques in the bedrooms, secluded gardens with pool and lily pond. **€€€.**

Villas and apartments
Prices vary enormously, according to the season and the luxuriousness of the accommodation. Prices may range from L800,000 per week for a simple four-person villa in the low season, to L4,000,000 for a magnificent secluded villa in the high season. These agencies arrange rentals:
American Agency, Via del Ponte Rosso 33r, 50129 Firenze, tel: 055-475053.
The Best in Italy, Via Ugo Foscolo 72, 50124 Firenze, tel: 055-223064, fax: 055-2298912. Run by Conte Brandolini d'Adda and offering villas or palazzi with pools, stables and other such luxuries.
Solemar, Via Cavour 80, 50129 Firenze, tel: 055-239361.
Casa Club, Via dei Termini 83, 53100 Siena, tel: 0577-44041.

Annalena, Via Romana 34, tel: 055-229600. Antique-furnished rooms in a gracious 15th-century former convent, built as a refuge for the widows of the Florentine nobility. Near the Giardino di Boboli, with views over a pretty garden. **€€.**
Aprile, Via della Scala 6, tel: 055-216237. More appealing than most hotels near the station, this is an ex-Medici palace, complete with frescoes, a pleasant breakfast room and garden. Rooms range from simple to quite grand, and prices vary accordingly. **€€.**
Beacci Tornabuoni Via dei Tornabuoni 3, tel: 055-212645. Set in a 14th-century palazzo with roof-garden in the city's most prestigious shopping street. Classically furnished. **€€.**

Calzaiuoli, Via del Calzaiuoli 6, tel: 055-212456. In a completely renovated mansion with origins dating back to the 14th century. Pleasant interiors, efficient service and great views from the upper floors. **€€.**

Le Due Fontane, Piazza Santissima Annunziata 14, tel: 055-210185. Small modern hotel located on a quiet, characterful square. Private parking. **€€.**

Il Guelfo Bianco, Via Cavour 57r, tel: 055-288330. Comfortably furnished rooms in two adjoining 15th-century houses just north of the Duomo. Spacious family rooms and a little internal courtyard. **€€.**

Loggiato Dei Serviti, Piazza Santissima Annunziata 3, tel: 055-289592. A small, friendly hotel in a 16th-century former monastery, opposite Brunelleschi's Ospedale degli Innocenti. Elegantly simple in style, with some antique furnishings. **€€.**

Mario's, Via Faenza 89, tel: 055-216801. Most of the hotels near the Mercato Centrale are pretty scruffy but Mario's is the exception. Decorated in rustic Tuscan style with comfortable bedrooms (the back is quieter). **€€.**

Torre Guelfa, Borgo SS Apostoli 8, tel: 055-2396338. This hotel includes the tallest privately-owned tower in Florence. The bedrooms are prettily furnished with smart bathrooms, and there is a grand salon. **€€.**

Campsites and youth hostels

The best-situated campsite, **Campeggio Italiani e Stranieri**, is under the Piazza Michelangelo, with room for 500 (Viale Michelangelo 80, tel: 055-6811977).

Youth hostels include: **Villa Camerata**, Viale Righi 2, tel: 055-601451 (also a campsite); **Santa Monaca**, Via Santa Monaca 6, tel: 055-268338; **Hostel Archi Rossi**, Via Faenza 94r, tel: 055-290804.

Alessandra, Borgo SS Apostoli 17, tel: 055-283438. Family-run hotel on the first floor of a 16th-century palazzo, next to the Uffizi and a short walk from the Ponte Vecchio. **€.**

Bretagna, Lungarno Corsini 6, tel: 055-289618. A beautiful villa beside the Arno (Louis Napoleon lived here for 10 years from 1820), with inlaid wooden floors and marble fireplaces. Sadly, only one room overlooks the Arno, but the river views from the enormous salon is a bonus. **€.**

Casci, Via Cavour 13, tel: 055-211686. Situated north of the San Lorenzo market area, this frescoed *quattrocentro* palazzo is family-run with a welcoming atmosphere. All bedrooms are air-conditioned. **€.**

Palazzo Vecchio, Via Cennini 4, tel: 055-212182. Right opposite the station, this surprisingly pleasant hotel has undergone a major renovation, and is comfortable and modern with good facilities for the price. Free parking. **€.**

Residenza Johlea, Via San Gallo 80, tel: 055-4633292. A delightful, small new hotel 10 minutes' walk north of the centre, offering great value for money. Only six bedrooms, elegantly decorated in pastel colours, and a stunning little roof-garden. **€.**

La Scaletta, Via Guicciardini 13, tel: 055-283028. In a convenient position near the Palazzo Pitti, this family-run *pensione* has a roof-garden, although some of the rooms are rather dowdy and not all have bathrooms. Half-board available. **€.**

Sorelli Bandini, Piazza Santo Spirito 9, tel. 055-215308. This hotel, rich in rather faded atmosphere, though rather lacking in comfort, is at the top of a palazzo on lively Piazza Santo Spirito. Delightful loggia. **€.**

Villa Le Rondine, Via Bolognese Vecchia 224, tel: 055-400081. Outside the centre, situated in lovely grounds, with a swimming pool in olive groves. **€.**

INDEX